Workers' Rights

MARY GIBSON

Rowman & Allanheld
PUBLISHERS

ROWMAN & ALLANHELD

Published in the United States of America in 1983
by Rowman & Allanheld, Publishers
(A division of Littlefield, Adams & Company)
81 Adams Drive, Totowa, New Jersey 07512

Library of Congress Cataloging in Publication Data

Gibson, Mary.
　Workers' rights.

　(Philosophy and society)
　Bibliography: p.
　Includes index.
　1. Employee rights—United States—Case studies.
2. Industrial hygiene—United States—Case studies.
3. Industrial safety—United States—Case studies.
4. Industrial relations—United States—Case studies.
I. Title. II. Series.
HD8072.5.G52　1983　　331'.01'1　　83-17788
ISBN 0-8476-6756-1

86 87　　9 8 7 6 5 4 3 2

Printed in the United States of America

SB　1810　10.95: 790

PHILOSOPHY AND SOCIETY
General Editor: Marshall Cohen

ALSO IN THIS SERIES:
RIGHTS
Theodore M. Benditt
ETHICS IN THE WORLD OF BUSINESS
David Braybrooke
MARX AND JUSTICE: *The Radical Critique of Liberalism*
Allen E. Buchanan
RONALD DWORKIN AND CONTEMPORARY JURISPRUDENCE
Marshall Cohen (ed.)
LUKÁCS, MARX AND THE SOURCES OF CRITICAL THEORY
Andrew Feenberg
THE REVERSE DISCRIMINATION CONTROVERSY
  A Moral and Legal Analysis
Robert Fullinwider
THE MORAL FOUNDATIONS OF PROFESSIONAL ETHICS
Alan H. Goldman
FEMINIST POLITICS AND HUMAN NATURE
Alison M. Jaggar
HANNAH ARENDT: POLITICS, CONSCIENCE, EVIL
George Kateb
PATERNALISM
John Kleinig
ECOLOGICAL ETHICS AND POLITICS
H. J. McCloskey
A PHILOSOPHY OF FREE EXPRESSION: *And Its Constitutional Applications*
Robert F. Ladenson
THE LIBERTARIAN READER
Tibor R. Machan (ed.)
MORAL PROBLEMS IN NURSING: *A Philosophical Investigation*
James L. Muyskens
READING NOZICK
Jeffrey Paul (ed.)
AND JUSTICE FOR ALL: *New Introductory Essays in Ethics and Public Policy*
Tom Regan and Donald VanDeVeer (eds.)
SEX, DRUGS, DEATH, AND THE LAW
  An Essay on Human Rights and Overcriminalization
David A. J. Richards
KANT'S POLITICAL PHILOSOPHY
Patrick Riley
EVOLUTIONARY EXPLANATION IN THE SOCIAL SCIENCES
  An Emerging Paradigm
Philippe Van Parijs
WELFARE RIGHTS
Carl Wellman

With love
to Julie, who helped me start down this path,
and Wells, who helps me every day to keep going.
Pass it on . . .

Contents

Preface   ix
Introduction   1
Chapter One   The Case of American Cyanamid   5
Chapter Two   The Case of Occidental Chemical   28
Chapter Three   The Case of the Burnside Foundry   57
Chapter Four   The Case of J. P. Stevens   87
Chapter Five   Rights   123
Notes   142
References   154
Index   163

Preface

This is in some ways a very ambitious book. It represents an attempt to combine concerns that many people are at pains to keep separate—the political and the academic-professional, the practical and the theoretical. It tries to speak not only to philosophers and academics in related disciplines, but to anyone who cares about the issues and is willing to think them through. It aims to be both useful and intellectually stimulating. It deals with a broad and complex subject matter that is relatively unfamiliar to most philosophers, and it attempts to stay firmly grounded in that subject matter.

Such an effort necessarily involves treading in areas where I have no special training nor expertise. So, at the same time that it is ambitious, this book is very modest. It makes no claims to being a definitive treatment of any aspect of the subject. It does not attempt to do social science or legal scholarship, despite the fact that it cannot avoid discussing matters that are considered to be the province of these disciplines. I apologize to those in the relevant disciplines for any oversimplifications that may have resulted. I do not, however, apologize for the absence of technical language or for not automatically accepting what may be considered standard assumptions in a given field. I hope I am equally guilty in my own discipline of these last two transgressions.

This book has been a long time in the making and I am indebted to too many people to be able to thank them all. I do, however, want to record some special debts.

I doubt that the book would ever have been written had not Marshall Cohen, as editor of this series, had sufficient faith in the project to make a commitment to it at a very early stage. His continued support and very helpful comments on drafts of each chapter encouraged me to keep going through periods of doubt and discouragement.

I want to thank Janet Johnston of Rowman & Allanheld for expertly shepherding the manuscript through the production process. I am grateful to Hy Cohen, copyeditor, for rescuing me from innumerable stylistic lapses and from a couple of substantive ones as well. Thanks also to art director Linda Holzman and production manager Tobi Krutt.

I want to thank all the other persons involved in the creation of the physical objects that will be this book—the indexer, typesetters, printers, binders, and whoever else is involved in the process. I regret that I cannot thank them by name because, I am told, there is no way of knowing, as I write this, who they will be.

Loretta Mandel typed the bulk of the manuscript—most of it several times—and offered extremely helpful comments and suggestions on the material she had typed. She also put in order a mess of bibliographical material. I also want to thank Rachel Sailer for the typing she did under difficult circumstances. Both Loretta and Rachel have been good friends through thick and thin.

Several times over the years, Marjorie Watson, a librarian at Rutgers University's Institute of Management & Labor Relations, has tracked down information that I had no idea how to locate. Her help has been invaluable.

The following people read and commented helpfully on preliminary materials or portions of the manuscript: Kathy Pyne Addelson, Virginia Held, Peter Klein, Barbara Lezynski, Howard McGary, Dot Nelkin, Amèlie Rorty, Tim Scanlon, Richard Schmitt, and Larry Stanton.

I especially want to thank Claudia Mills, Robert Fullinwider, and Wells Keddie: Claudia, for checking my work to make sure I was getting it right; Bob for trying to pound sense into my head; and Wells, for trying to make sure I didn't betray the working class. I hope they met with some success.

I benefited from a semester's leave under Rutgers University's Faculty Academic Study Program and from two Rutgers University Research Council grants to help defray expenses. I also want to acknowledge the Rutgers University administration and some of my colleagues on the Rutgers faculty for providing me with some very relevant first-hand experience while I was working on this book. I learned what it is like to be fired from a job after nine years in the position, and to spend two years in the grievance process trying—so far unsuccessfully—to get the job back. I do want to thank the many friends and colleagues who have been supportive during this time, and especially those who stuck their necks out in various ways to help defend my rights.

INTRODUCTION

It don't stop. It just goes and goes and goes. I bet there's men who have lived and died out there, never seen the end of that line. And they never will—because it's endless. It's like a serpent. It's just all body, no tail. It can do things to you. . . .

I don't understand how come more guys don't flip. Because you're nothing more than a machine when you hit this type of thing. They give better care to that machine than they will to you. They'll have more respect, give more attention to that machine. And you know this. Somehow you get the feeling that the machine is better than you are [laughter].

You really begin to wonder. What price do they put on me? Look at the price they put on the machine. If that machine breaks down, there's somebody out there to fix it right away. If I break down, I'm just pushed over to the other side till another man takes my place. The only thing they have on their mind is to keep that line running.

—*Phil Stallings, spot-welder*
(from Working *by Studs Terkel)*

This is a book about workers, the problems they face and the rights for which they have struggled—and, as we shall see, must continue to struggle. Each of the first four chapters begins with the presentation of a particular problem confronting real workers in a real workplace. In each chapter, then, the practical and philosophical issues discussed are those raised by an actual predicament in which workers have recently found themselves.

One of the advantages of using real cases is their richness. In any given case, several different issues are almost certain to arise and to affect one another in a variety of ways. Unfortunately, besides making things interesting, this can make discussion of the issues frustratingly difficult and complex. Indeed, the main beauty of hypothetical cases, of which philosophers are so notoriously fond, is that they can be tailored in such a way as to isolate an issue that one wants to focus on, eliminating most of the complicating factors that might distort or obscure the issue or blunt one's intuitions. But isolating issues in this way has serious drawbacks as well. The complexities of real cases may distort our perception of the issues, but isolating the issues may distort our perception of reality. Issues come interrelated in the social contexts in which they arise and have impact on real people's lives. How they are related and how they interact may be among the most important things about them. Thus it is hoped that the use of real cases will prove illuminating in two ways. Philosophical discussion may bring some useful clarity to our understanding of the practical problems described. At the same time, seeing the philosophical issues in the context of the practical everyday situations in which they arise may shed some light on those issues.

The first chapter begins with the case of five women who were required to have themselves surgically sterilized in order to retain their jobs, which involved exposure to lead. The employer's reason for this requirement was that exposure to lead could be harmful to potential offspring. Among the many issues intertwined in this case are reproductive rights, paternalism, privacy, discrimination, "protective" policies, and the right of all workers to a safe and healthful workplace. These are the issues discussed in Chapter One.

In Chapter Two, we discuss the problems faced by male chemical workers who discovered that they had been sterilized in the course of their work producing the pesticide DBCP, which they had not been warned was potentially harmful. This case overlaps with the first on several issues, but raises specifically the issue of workers' right to know the nature and potential hazards of the substances they work with. We explore the general informational requirements for informed consent to workplace hazards and the relation of the right-to-know issue to the issue of control of the workplace.

A fatal explosion in a steel foundry opens Chapter Three. Days earlier, several workers had been sent home for refusing to work in the area until pools of water on the floor were removed. They knew that if the water were contacted by the molten steel they were pouring, an explosion would ensue. The hazard was not corrected and several workers lost their lives. In discussing this case, we argue that an effective right to refuse an unsafe assignment is another necessary condition for informed consent to workplace hazards. Noting that the right to refuse is empty if refusing can cost one's job—or if one does not have a job—we go on to explore the claim that persons have a right to a job. We observe that the considerations which support the claim that they do also support the claim that they have a right to useful and challenging work.

The years-long battle by textile workers at a J. P. Stevens plant for union recognition and a union contract is described in the opening pages of Chapter Four. The issues discussed here include the right of workers to organize and bargain collectively, the right to strike, union security versus "right-to-work" laws, racial and sexual discrimination in the workplace, and the apparent inability or unwillingness of the courts and responsible agencies to protect the rights of workers. The discussion is rounded out by consideration of the rights of union members within their unions.

In these chapters, then, starting from the concrete situations in which workers find themselves and exploring the ramifications of and interconnections among the issues raised by them, we are led to consider topics ranging from sterilization abuse to the free-rider problem, from labeling of hazardous substances to workers' control, from plant closings to autonomy.

Finally, in Chapter Five, we discuss directly the concept of rights that is largely taken for granted in the first four chapters. This chapter is necessarily somewhat more abstract than the others. In it I sketch what I think of as an essentially Marxian account of the nature, functions, and limits of rights. Some account of these matters is owed to the reader of a book that makes such heavy use of a concept as controversial and variously interpreted as that of rights.

We observe in Chapters One through Four that the rights of workers are, in many important ways, not satisfied under existing laws and procedures in the United States. We may be led by the discussion in Chapter Five to ask whether it is possible fully to satisfy them within the framework of our current economic and political system. That system faces a challenge: It must show itself capable of satisfying the rights to which it gives rise, or it must be condemned, not—or not only—by some external standard, but in its own terms, by the very ideals of rights and justice which it has engendered and embraced.

A few words about neutrality and objectivity are in order. First, as will be evident in what follows, I neither aim nor claim to be neutral about the issues discussed in this book. This is partly because I am, as a matter of fact, not neutral on these matters; also, and more important, because I do not believe that neutrality is either possible or desirable. Thus I want to distinguish neutrality from objectivity, for which I do strive. One does not have to be on the fence concerning an issue in order to be objective about it. Indeed, if one side in the issue has, objectively, a much stronger case than the other, it will be difficult or impossible for a person who is well informed about the issue to be both objective and neutral.

Precisely what objectivity consists of and whether it can ever fully be achieved are important and difficult philosophical questions that I cannot address here. This much, however, can be said. Objectivity involves an openness to the facts and a willingness to explore, as far as possible, the implications of one's views. If the facts cannot be reconciled with one's views, or if the logical implications of one's views are untenable, objectivity requires at least that one recognize that there must be errors within one's set of relevant beliefs, seek to find the errors, and revise one's views accordingly.

This is not to say that "the facts" come to us pure and transparent, uncolored by the views, theories, assumptions, attitudes, and habits of thought that, consciously or unconsciously, we already have. That the facts are theory-laden in various ways does not, however, entail thoroughgoing relativism or skepticism. We are often able to see that we have been wrong about something. And often people with very different beliefs, theories, and world-views are able to agree on many of the facts. Even if objectivity must always be a matter of degree, in any particular instance, that degree may be perfectly adequate for the purposes at hand.

Some people who agree that objectivity is possible with regard to matters of fact hold that there can be no such thing as objectivity concerning matters of value. On this view, there is a fundamental distinction between facts and values: the former are objective and susceptible to empirical, scientific discovery and confirmation; the latter are subjective and normative, determined by cultural conditioning and individual taste or preference. It is an objective matter what someone's values are, according to this view, but not whether those values are good or bad, or whether statements expressing value judgments are true or false. But to say that a person is harmed if her hand is mangled in a machine, or if he loses eighty percent of his breathing capacity, is to express a value judgment. It is also to state an objective fact. To say that one person has exploited or taken unfair advantage of another is to make a statement that is at once normative and empirical—a statement the truth or falsity of which is, in principle and often in practice, objectively determinable. The idea that normative judgments cannot be objective seems mistaken.

I suspect that people are drawn to the view just described not so much by its own plausibility as by the implausibility of what is often taken to be the only alternative. It seems to be widely held that if values are to be objective, they must somehow be absolute and eternally fixed. I believe, on the contrary, that it is possible—consistently—to be a historicist and an objectivist. I cannot here defend this admittedly controversial position. Chapter Five may be seen as, not a defense, but a partial development and illustration of this general view in terms of my specific views on the nature of rights, which I take to be at once normative, historical, and objective.

One

The Case of American Cyanamid

Workers' rights must be examined in terms of the concrete realities of the everyday lives of real human beings. The following newspaper article describes the choice that was thrust upon women workers in West Virginia: to be sterilized or to lose their jobs. This story raises compelling issues concerning the rights of workers: the right of workers to a safe and healthful workplace, reproductive rights, privacy, paternalism, protective policies, discrimination. These are the issues that will be explored in this chapter.

WILLOW ISLAND, W. Va.—The giant American Cyanamid Corp. has what could be described only as a corporate public relations nightmare on its hands here.

What began a year ago as a drive, according to the chemical conglomerate's spokesmen, to shift its female employees out of positions at the company's plant here where exposure to lead could harm their unborn children has backfired into charges by five of the women that they had to get themselves surgically sterilized to hang onto their jobs.

The women, who range in age from 26 to 43, said in interviews that they reluctantly allowed themselves to be sterilized at a local hospital only after they were pressured to get the operations by American Cyanamid officials at the company's Ohio River chemical complex.

Two other women who did not have operations were transferred out of the plant's pigment division into lesser-paying janitor's jobs in October.

The entire 17-women component of the company's production force here has sought advice on what to do next from a local lawyer and their union, the Oil, Chemical and Atomic Workers, has vowed to make their case a national issue.

"These women were forced to make a Draconian choice that nobody should have to make," said Anthony Mazzocchi, the union's vice president. "It's an outrageous situation and American Cyanamid is not the only company that is trying to force women out of the workplace rather than clean it up," said Mazzocchi. "Women who have been able to enter these jobs as a result of their own struggle are now being confronted with the dismal choice of relinquishing their right to have children or their jobs."

Spokesmen for the chemical company emphatically denied that American Cyanamid was responsible for the sterilization of the women. They said the policy was aimed solely at protecting unborn children.

"Our doctor met with all of the women in September when our policy was announced," said a spokesman here. "At that time we said that we discourage sterilization and that if it was done we did not sanction it."

A spokesman at the firm's corporate headquarters in Wayne, N.J., said, "from a moral point of view the company feels it is on the side of the angels in this thing." . . .

Other firms, such as General Motors, reportedly have refused to assign women to jobs with lead exposure and the policy has drawn fire from women's groups. The Equal Employment Opportunity Commission has also indicated that such blanket exclusionary policies could violate federal civil rights laws. In 1977, American Cyanamid tried to bar women from jobs with harmful chemicals at its Linden, N.J., plant but the company dropped its policy after opposition from the United Steelworkers.

In the American Cyanamid situation here, however, the company's spokesmen claim the case against lead is so well documented that they decided to restrict all women workers under 50 with childbearing capacity to two sections of the plant where no lead is used.

. . . Women in the plant said they were told by company officials at the time that the policy eventually would be expanded to cover all but the two non-lead departments "within a few months."

Last January, the women were told during two meetings with plant officials in Willow Island that some of the chemicals at the plant and lead were potentially dangerous to pregnant women and that their jobs would be shifted.

"They told us we could go to the janitorial department but that if there weren't enough jobs there some of us might have to leave," said Betty Moler, one of the women who was sterilized. Janitorial department workers make less money and have less chance for overtime, she said.

Moler and the other women interviewed said the two departments left open to the women for transfer out of the janitorial department were both staffed with men with seniority over them and with no openings. All the women said that company officials pressured them directly or indirectly to accept sterilization.

In an interview at her home in Belmont near here Moler, who is 27 and has one son, said she told company officials her husband already had had a vasectomy. She was told, she said, that did not matter.

Another of the women, Lola Rymer, 43, said they offered to sign papers so the company would not be held liable for any lead exposure problems. That was also rejected, she said.

The women all said they went ahead with the operations because of pressure from company officials and because they stood to lose several thousand dollars in overtime pay if they shifted jobs.

The company's lead policy apparently contradicts federal regulations on the metal which were issued in October by the Occupational Safety and Health Administration.

The new regulations cut the allowable level of airborne lead in the workplace to 50 micrograms per cubic meter of air from the former 200 microgram level. In addition, the regulations set a 30 microgram "action level" at which a company must initiate special monitoring. The regulations warn of possible neurological damage to a fetus at lead levels above 30 micrograms and to all adults at over a 50 microgram reading.

The new regulations were strongly opposed by the lead industry, including American Cyanamid.

Supposedly, if the regulations are followed there should be no harm to a fetus. "Given the data in this record," the regulations state, "OSHA believes there is no basis whatsoever for the claim that women of childbearing age should be excluded from the workplace in order to protect the fetus."

American Cyanamid declined requests from The Washington Post to be allowed to see the company's measurements of lead dust in the air of the pigment section, where paint is mixed. The company also refused to allow photographs of the area. [Washington Post–LA Times News Service, printed in *Home News*, New Brunswick, N.J. January 3, 1979.]

Lead

Lead poisoning was first recognized as an occupational disease when lead miners suffered from it in ancient times (Stellman, 1977, 178). There are two kinds of lead, inorganic and organic (or tetraethyl) lead. Both are highly toxic, though their effects are somewhat different.

Inorganic lead is typically found in pigments and in grinding operations. It enters the body mainly through inhalation, and is stored in the bones, where it affects the blood-forming tissue in the bone marrow. Chronic exposure results in insomnia, fatigue, constipation, anemia, colic, neuritis, tremors, headache, loss of appetite, weakness, double vision, brain damage (sometimes severe enough to cause permanent retardation in children), high blood pressure and kidney failure.

Organic lead is found mainly in leaded gasoline. It is readily absorbed through the skin; its other main route of entry is inhalation. It is stored in the brain, resulting in mental disturbance, insomnia, anxiety, and (from acute exposure) delirium and death.

The body stores lead of both kinds for extremely long periods of time, so the effects of repeated exposure are cumulative. Medical

treatments for lead poisoning exist, but they are themselves dangerous, and their effectiveness is not established (Stellman and Daum,
1973, 252–53).

Of 102 children of lead smelter workers in Tennessee tested for lead
absorption levels, fifty were found to have excessive absorption,
presumably from lead brought home on their parents' clothing. Such
poisoning (sometimes fatal) of spouses and children of occupationally
exposed workers is not uncommon and has been seen with other
substances, such as asbestos and beryllium, as well as with lead.
Chronic lead poisoning in children can often show up as hyperactiv-
ity among other more severe disturbances.

Reproductive effects of lead exposure include high rates of miscar-
riage and stillbirth (both for women directly exposed and for wives of
exposed men), reduced male libido and fertility (prolonged exposure
can result in atrophy of testes), and sperm abnormalities. Lead is
known to be capable of crossing the placental barrier and entering
fetal blood and tissue, and animal tests suggest that it is teratogenic
(capable of causing birth defects as a result of such fetal exposure).
There is also evidence of genetic damage, making it a suspected
mutagen. Mutagens, of course, can act through both males and
females.

Discussion

Among the many issues involved in this case are (a) the right of all
workers to a safe and heathful workplace (guaranteed by the Occupational Safety and Health Act of 1970); (b) discrimination; (c) protective
policies; (d) privacy; (e) reproductive rights; (f) informed consent; and
(g) paternalism.

Here I shall discuss these issues primarily in relation to the case at
hand. I shall explore some of the ways in which they are intertwined,
raise many questions, suggest (and to varying degrees defend) a few
answers, and present some views and arguments propounded by
others. My purpose here is not so much to establish any particular
conclusions, as to begin to explore the situation in its complexity and
thus to provide grist for other mills. Insofar as my own views,
intuitions and convictions may also serve as grist, I offer them in that
spirit, with no pretensions of having argued for them in a fully
rigorous or systematic way. If they are provocative, they will have
done their job. If they are convincing, so much the better.

In the first four chapters, we shall be operating with a common-
sense notion of (moral) rights such that (a) some rights may exist

independently of whether they are recognized or guaranteed by law (though in some cases, if they exist they ought to be so recognized); (b) legal recognition or guarantee does not establish—though it suggests, and may even serve as evidence—that the legal right is also, reflects, or corresponds to, a moral right (Some legal rights may be incompatible with important moral rights. If so, the former probably ought not to exist in their present form. This says nothing about possible conflicts between existing moral rights.); (c) some moral rights may be created or established by the existence of corresponding or other legal rights or circumstances. For the most part I shall simply assume the existence of the various rights that come up in the course of discussion in these first four chapters.

The purpose of the Occupational Safety and Health Act (the OSH Act) of 1970 is, in its own words, "to assure so far as possible every working man and woman in the nation safe and healthful working conditions and to preserve our human resources," and to "assure insofar as practicable that no employee shall suffer diminished health, functional capacity or life expectancy as a result of his work experience." In what is known as the "general duty clause," the act states that each employer "shall furnish to each of his employees employment and a place of employment which are free from recognized hazards that are causing or are likely to cause death or serious physical harm to his employees."

The phrases "as far as possible," and "insofar as practicable," leave room for wide differences as to what the act requires in cases that are not covered by more specific standards (as well as over how the specific standards themselves should be determined). Employers generally interpret these phrases as mandating that "economic feasibility" or cost-benefit studies be conducted prior to setting any specific standards. These studies are misleading at best since, typically, the costs of illness and injury that are taken into account are the costs to the employer for compensation and disability, not the costs to the worker and his or her family in lost wages (those workers who receive compensation at all receive on the average slightly over one fifth of what their wages would have been [Berman, 1978, 62]) much less the pain and suffering and loss of life itself. Thus, the worse the compensation a diseased or injured worker (or a dead worker's family) receives, the higher the *relative* cost of prevention, whatever the actual dollar cost of prevention may be, and hence the lower the "economic feasibility" of prevention. Nor are social costs such as welfare and foodstamps for disabled workers and their families taken into account, still less costs in potential harm to future generations.

Moreover, even if one wanted to include consideration of these costs, among the most important of them are noneconomic ones (pain, suffering, loss of life, bereavement), and there is no appropriate way of comparing them with the financial costs of cleaning up the workplace. Controversy over the role of economic feasibility or cost-benefit studies is one of many ongoing battles in the efforts of the Occupational Safety and Health Administration (OSHA) to carry out the mandate of the OSH Act.[1]

While the legal right to a safe and healthful workplace may be subject to various interpretations and rulings based on technicalities, loopholes, enforcement difficulties, claims of ruinous effects on industry, etc., the right that the law seems clearly intended to recognize and protect is the right not to be exposed to unnecessary risks to life, safety or health for the sake of greater convenience or profit for the employer—and not to be forced to choose between accepting the risks and forfeiting the job.

In view of the harmful effects of lead on exposed adults (diminished health, in the language of the OSH Act) and of its known and suspected reproductive effects on both men and women (functional capacity), it seems clear that the exclusion of fertile women from high lead exposure jobs involves, in one way or another, violation of the rights of all of the workers involved. Workers remaining on the job face health and reproductive risks that violate their rights under the OSH Act; the women who are sterilized to keep their jobs are forced to accept diminished functional capacity as a condition of employment, while the health risks to themselves remain substantially as before. And the women excluded from the jobs have their rights against sex discrimination, as provided by Title VII of the Civil Rights Act and Executive Order No. 11246, violated. (Title VII of the Civil Rights Act of 1964, as amended by the Equal Employment Opportunity Act of 1972, provides that no one shall be discriminated against on the basis of sex, race, color, or national origin in the area of employment. Executive Order No. 11246 forbids discrimination in employment by the federal government and by federal government contractors.)

Let us look briefly now at the reproductive and privacy rights involved in this case. Reproductive rights are not yet generally spelled out in law in the United States. The legal status of abortion has been treated as a matter of the right of privacy, specifically in the relation between a woman and her physician. More generally one would expect reproductive rights and privacy rights to overlap extensively, especially in a society where reproductive decisions and activities are considered among the most personal and private aspects of life, and are thought to be at the core of what is called the private sphere. It seems to me unlikely that reproductive rights can be entirely reduced to or subsumed under privacy rights. Still, persons who may be skeptical about reproductive rights could object to the Cyanamid policy on privacy grounds. The Department of Health, Education and Welfare (now the Department of Health and Human Services) has, as of March 8, 1979, regulations governing federal financial participation in sterilization programs which establish certain rights and protections against involuntary sterilization in federally funded programs. The application of these regulations is, of course, limited, but they may be seen as expressing recognition of certain reproductive rights. Thus, while the existence of reproductive rights seems to be fairly widely acknowledged today, there is no official or widely recognized statement, definition or interpretation of those rights. For present purposes, let me suggest that reproductive rights involve, among other things, the right to make one's own decisions about whether and when to have children and at what risk (there are always some risks), and about how best to carry out those decisions—whether by use of contraceptives and if so by which method, or by sterilization and if so of which partner and by which method, whether to abort an unplanned pregnancy or one involving special risks to mother or child, etc. If this is even approximately correct, it seems clear that American Cyanamid's policy violated the reproductive rights of the sterilized women, and I suggest it did so in an area where reproductive and privacy rights overlap, thus violating their rights to privacy as well.

Two objections are likely to arise. First, it may be objected that the company was only doing the responsible thing—that it would be irresponsible to allow the women to continue working at those jobs when they might become pregnant (recall the company spokesman's statement that, "from a moral point of view the company feels it is on the side of the angels in this thing"). Second, it may be objected that the women were not deprived of the right to make their own decisions: they could have chosen to give up their jobs.

Let us consider the first objection. Employers offer the following arguments for the claim that exclusion of fertile women from certain jobs is justified: a woman may become pregnant even if she doesn't intend to; pregnancy is often not discovered for several weeks and the early weeks of pregnancy are the period of greatest fetal susceptibility to teratogens; exposure levels safe for adults may still be dangerous to fetuses; thus the morally responsible policy is to protect the potential offspring. This is best achieved by the exclusion of fertile women because reduction of exposure levels sufficient to ensure safety of the fetus is often economically or technologically unfeasible; and finally, exclusion affects negligible numbers of women, since few are employed in the industries in question. (*Women's Occupational Health Resource Center News*, 1979; Lehmann, undated, 4–5)

This objection does not deny that the policy restricts reproductive freedom, rather it claims that under the circumstances such restriction is justified.

In response to this claim, it is worth noting that our society generally leaves to the individual parents decisions about risks to potential children. As Joan Bertin of the American Civil Liberties Union notes:

> Women workers are being required to make this agonizing decision even where the "risk" associated with their employment is wholly speculative or less, for example, than that posed by drinking coffee or alcoholic beverages or smoking cigarettes. The risk they face is surely less than that faced daily by couples with known genetic or other characteristics which increase the chance that their children may be born with Down's Syndrome, hemophilia, Tay-Sachs disease, sickle cell disease, Huntington's Chorea, or similar condition. Yet in all these situations, it is the right of the parents to choose. Why should it be different for women workers? [Bertin, 1982, 216]

Consistency seems to require that the right to make one's own reproductive choices be treated the same in the workplace as it is elsewhere in our society—or that a justification be given for differential treatment.

In any event, whether or not our first objector claims that the sterilization-or-exclusion policy constitutes (a) a (justified) violation, or (b) no violation of reproductive rights will depend on whether he or she holds (a) that rights that are overridden are (justifiably) violated, or (b) that to say that an act or policy violates a right carries with it the claim that the act or policy is unjustified, as well as on (c) whether she or he holds that there are reproductive rights of the sort proposed above. These are not questions we need to—or can—settle here.

The justifiability of the sterilization-or-exclusion policy, then, may depend, entirely or to some degree, on whether or not the relevant reproductive rights exist and on their relative weight vis-a-vis the considerations raised in favor of the policy. In this case, the objector cannot show conclusively that the policy is justified without settling these difficult and controversial matters. We might, however, be able to decide, on other grounds, that the policy is unjustified or that its justification is at best doubtful. In assessing whether the policy ought to be adopted, all things considered, the possibility that it would violate reproductive rights could, then, count as an additional consideration against it.

Let us turn now to the second objection—that the women were not deprived of the right to make their own decisions because they could have chosen to give up their jobs rather than be sterilized. This objection raises important and difficult questions about the relative freedom or coerciveness of various choices and choice situations. Some of these questions arise in relation to choices concerning terms and conditions of employment in general, and thus connect directly with the question of whether the employment contract is ever the result of a voluntary agreement between equal parties in a free and open market. In various ways almost everything in this book is relevant to this general issue, so I will not attempt to address it directly here. In relation to the particular case at hand, it might be argued, in support of the claim that the women's reproductive rights were violated, that there is a fairly strong similarity between this case and cases where women are told they must "consent" to be sterilized or lose their eligibility for welfare and/or medicaid benefits. This practice is now widely condemned as sterilization abuse and a clear violation of reproductive rights. It is expressly prohibited in the recently adopted Health and Human Services (H & HS) regulations for federally funded sterilization programs mentioned above. In such cases, this argument goes, consent is not genuine, even though the person has chosen between two (unattractive) alternatives.

But, our objector may respond, a person can be forced to choose among unattractive alternatives by circumstances that are beyond anyone's control, and it does not seem correct to say that consent is always lacking in such cases. For example, following an accident, if a person forced to choose between having a leg amputated and almost certain death decides on the amputation, it is appropriate to say he or she was forced to choose amputation, or even that he or she had no choice. But this surely does not imply that she or he did not genuinely consent to the operation.

The point is well taken. This suggests that we must distinguish between being *forced* and being *coerced*. The genuineness of consent is undermined by coercion but not (at least not always) by force-of-circumstances. The kinds of sterilization abuse prohibited by H & HS are objectionable because they are coercive. Was the Cyanamid policy coercive?

Several different accounts of coercion have been offered by philoso-phers over the past dozen or so years, so the answer to this question is likely to be controversial.[2] It does seem clear, however, that coerciveness is often a matter of degree. To the degree, then, that the company coerced the women by requiring them to choose between their jobs and their fertility, to that degree their reproductive rights were violated. To that degree the women who were sterilized were sterilized without their genuine consent. And to that degree the policy may be seen as sterilization abuse.

That degree seems to me to be substantial, especially in view of the alternative that could have been made available to them and was not: that the dangers be fully and accurately presented to them, steps be taken to minimize exposure of all workers as far as possible, remain-ing exposure levels be carefully monitored and the workers informed of them, and then the women decide for themselves whether to remain in the division, and if so, whether to have themselves steril-ized.

In addition, to the extent that coercion involves *preventing* someone from having a preferred alternative, it seems worth noting that the distinction between *preventing* someone's having such an alternative and *not helping* someone to have it is not always clear.[3] Where this is the case, the distinction between being coerced and being forced by circumstances will also be blurred. This is so especially where pat-terns of action and inaction of many persons acting more or less independently result in the unavailability of the preferred alternative. To a large extent these patterns are themselves the results, not necessarily intended, of other human decisions and actions which create and maintain the framework of social institutions, expecta-tions, and attitudes within which the previously mentioned actions and inactions occur. Whether or not we decide to say that situations in which persons are forced to choose among alternatives restricted by such patterns of action and inaction are coercive, let us say that a person in such a situation is at least less free than she or he might be. And where human action could alter the patterns and/or frameworks so that the preferred alternative(s) could be made available, such a person is unnecessarily unfree. Clearly both of these—freedom or lack of it and necessity or lack of it—will be matters of degree.[4] Nevertheless, where the degrees are high enough, we may want to say that persons ought not to be unnecessarily unfree in certain ways. And, since freedom is a good, this would be a reason for acting to provide the preferred alternative even independently of whether not providing it violated rights.

Let us turn now to discussion of the interrelated issues of protective policies, paternalism and discrimination.

To bring out some of the ways in which these issues are, or may be related, we can set forth the following general questions, which it will be useful to keep in mind during the course of the discussion, though it is doubtful that any of them will be conclusively answered:

1. When, if ever, are protective policies paternalistic?
2. When, if ever, are protective policies discriminatory?
3. When, if ever, are protective policies protective?
4. How are the answers to 1–3 related to each other?

The history of protectionism, that is of special labor laws or policies applying only to women, purportedly to protect them from certain job hazards, is complex and paradoxical. Male workers sometimes supported "protective" policies in order to prevent women from entering certain occupations, competing for "men's" jobs, and depressing wages. That the restricted kinds of jobs available to women forced them to accept lower wages, and that men often did not recruit or even admit women into their unions so that they could command higher wages, made this a vicious cycle. Thus, some women opposed all protective policies as mere rationalizations for discrimination. Yet conditions were so bad that some women accepted the restrictions, welcoming whatever relief they could get. And protective legislation, defended on sexist and discriminatory grounds, has in several instances paved the way for significant improvements in conditions for all workers. One example is the ten-hour day.[5]

In general, in response to question 2 above, it seems to me that protective policies are discriminatory and unjustifiable. If job conditions are such that women should be protected from them, then men should be protected as well. Whether there are any exceptions to this general rule is a more difficult question, one to which we shall return specifically in connection with exclusionary policies.

Let us turn now to paternalism. For purposes of this discussion, we shall adopt what has come to be the standard philosophical conception of paternalism, i.e., what John Stuart Mill argues against in *On Liberty* and Gerald Dworkin discusses in his essay, "Paternalism." Later on we shall explore a somewhat different way of thinking about paternalism, but for now let us proceed on the basis of Dworkin's characterization: "By paternalism I shall understand roughly the interference with a person's liberty of action justified by reasons referring exclusively to the welfare, good, happiness, needs, interests or values of the person being coerced" (G. Dworkin, 1971, 108).

A note of clarification: The word "justify" may be used in two different ways. On one usage, to say that an act or policy is justified by certain reasons is to say that the act or policy is, in fact, justified. On another usage, to say that an act or policy is justified (by an agent) by reference to certain reasons does not imply that those reasons actually suffice to justify the act or policy in question. The reasons are offered as justification, but the attempted justification may or may not succeed. It seems that we must understand Dworkin, in the passage just quoted, to be using the term in the latter way. For if it is taken in the former way, there could be no such thing as *un*justified paternalism, and this clearly is not his intention.

Without pausing to discuss the many substantive difficulties involved, let me suggest for now that paternalism, in Dworkin's sense, may be (actually) justified in some cases where it is necessary to preserve or expand the freedom or autonomy of the individual in question. Dworkin makes a similar suggestion and proposes some guidelines intended to place the burden of proof on those who would impose paternalistic measures (G. Dworkin, 1971, 118–26). His proposal seems likely to permit a far wider range of paternalism than I think justifiable, but the basic approach seems correct. What is striking, though, when one looks at actual cases where the issue of paternalism arises, is how very rare genuine instances of paternalism, as characterized in the preceding paragraph, seem to be.[6] Thus, to the question whether or not the apparent paternalism in a particular case is justified, there is the prior question of whether it is indeed an instance of paternalism in the relevant sense.

Let us consider, then, whether our example counts as a case involving paternalism at all. Assuming the conception of paternalism characterized above, there are at least two reasons why it might be said not to. First, it might be said that the policy is not paternalistic because it is aimed, not at the good of the women employees, but at the prevention of harm to their potential offspring. Second, it might be claimed that the policy is not paternalistic because, despite initial appearances, it is not motivated solely (if at all) by consideration of the good of the potential mothers *or* children, but by the company's concern to protect itself against potential lawsuits by or on behalf of damaged offspring.

Let us first consider the claim that the policy is not paternalistic in that it is not aimed at the good of the women but at the prevention of harm to their potential offspring. The policy is analogous to the prohibition of abortion for protection of the fetus (rather than of the pregnant woman—which was in fact the stated motivation for much of the original anti-abortion legislation in the United States), or interventions to prevent or stop child abuse, or to permit needed medical treatment for a child whose parents refuse permission. All of these cases involve intervention in an area normally thought to be the domain of the parent(s) or pregnant woman. The intervention is based, however, on consideration of the good, needs or interests of the child or fetus, which parents or potential parents are normally counted on to promote, but which are seen as threatened in these instances. Such intervention may or may not be justified. But it is not paternalism, either justified or unjustified, according to the claim under discussion. (If this claim is correct, the question still remains whether the policy in question is an acceptable way of preventing the harm in question; that depends, among other things, on what alternatives are available—but more on this below.)

One possible response to this claim is that, at least in our society, parents are generally thought not merely to promote the interests of their children, but to share those interests, to take them as their own.[7] John Rawls expresses this idea in his theory of justice by treating the parties to the social contract as continuing chains of interests extending at least through two generations (Rawls, 1971, 128f). In light of this, it is at least not obviously inappropriate to call any of the interventions mentioned above paternalistic (in Dworkin's sense).

Also, it is worth noting that, if the Cyanamid policy is not paternalistic for the reason given, then much if not all "protective" legislation in the U.S. has been nonpaternalistic. Historically, the arguments for "protective" regulations, such as prohibition of heavy lifting and of long or late hours typically appealed not only (if at all) to women's physical weakness and dependency, but also to their "maternal function," maintaining that special protections were needed in order to preserve the species, the family, and moral values. For example, a spokesman for the American Federation of Labor said in 1900, "Women may be adults, and why should we class them as children? Because it is to the interest of all of us that female labor should be limited so as not to injure the motherhood and family life of a nation" (Milkman, 1980, 122).[8] It may, of course, be correct to say that none of these "protective" policies should count as paternalistic (at least in Dworkin's sense). This would support the views of those who have argued all along that "protective" policies do not protect or benefit women, but discriminate against them.

The second reason for denying that our example involves paternalism was that the policy is not motivated by consideration of the good of the potential mothers or children, but by the company's concern to protect itself against potential lawsuits by or on behalf of damaged offspring. Such cases, this reasoning holds, involve self-interest (justified or not) which has the appearance (intended or not) of paternalism (justified or not). Even unjustified paternalism often looks better than self-interest.

A possible response to this point is that it is not the motivation but the justification of an act or policy that makes it paternalistic. According to Dworkin, paternalistic interference is *"justified* by reasons referring exclusively to the welfare, good," etc., of the person coerced (emphasis added).

But it seems unlikely that Dworkin intends, or that the generally accepted philosophical understanding of paternalism involves, a clear-cut distinction between motivation and justification such that the motives of the agent would have nothing to do with whether or not an act or policy was paternalistic. We want to be able to distinguish between cases of genuine paternalism and cases where paternalistic-sounding reasons are mere window-dressing. This distinction is presupposed by the claim under consideration, according to which Cyanamid's expressed concern for the potential fetuses is really window-dressing. And it does not appear that we can preserve this distinction if we treat the agent's motivation as irrelevant to determining whether an act or policy is genuinely paternalistic.

Moreover, the relevance of motivation seems inescapable when we recognize the possibility of self-deception on the part of those who are in a position to impose restrictions upon others "for their own good." Too often such restrictions actually advance the interests of those imposing them, often at the expense of the purported beneficiaries, even though this is not perceived by the agents. Perceptions are notoriously influenced by interests. The strength of this tendency is one reason why many people are reluctant to allow that paternalism is ever permissible. The difficulty of determining in practice when an agent's reasons are genuinely paternalistic and when they are self-deceptive (mirror-dressing as well as window-dressing) may be good reason for being suspicious of paternalism. But the conceptual difference is a real and important one, at least on the conception of paternalism we have been using in this discussion. And I do not see how it can be preserved without involving motivations.

Thus, although this discussion is inconclusive, I remain sympathetic to the view that the Cyanamid policy was not paternalistic in Dworkin's sense because it was not really motivated by concern for the potential mothers or their children.

Why, it may be asked, am I so skeptical about the company's

motives? Granted that self-interest may have had a role in their decision, might not genuine concern over potential harm to the unborn have been involved too? Of course, as we noted above, it is often difficult or impossible to tell in practice what really motivates an agent. But there are, it seems to me, fairly strong reasons for skepticism in this case.

Excessive lead exposure is known to be extremely harmful to adult men and women, and to their already existing children. Moreover, lead is known to affect the male as well as the female reproductive system. Why, then, Cyanamid's single-minded effort to exclude fertile women from lead exposure areas while willfully exposing other workers to excessive levels (see *Update*, at end of chapter)? As Jeanne Stellman notes in her excellent book, *Women's Work, Women's Health*, "There seems to be an aura of sanctity about a fertilized egg, a sort of fetus fetish, that apparently disappears when a child is born or matures into a working person" (Stellman, 1977, 179–80). Why so much concern about the unborn and so little about the living?

The most plausible explanation has two related parts: (1) potential costs of law suits to the company, and (2) stereotyped and discriminatory attitudes toward women and reproduction.

Under present state workers' compensation laws there are fixed, and usually very low, maximum limits on the rates to be paid for any occupationally caused injury or disease. They do not permit employees covered by workers' compensation to sue their employers in cases of occupationally related illness or injury. In cases of disease, such as those associated with lead poisoning (in contrast to clear-cut injuries, such as having one's hand mangled in a machine) they generally place the burden of proof on the worker to establish that the condition was caused by his or her job, and not by personal habits or lifestyle (e.g., smoking), general environmental exposure to toxins, or the "normal aging process." Thus the potential cost to the company resulting from lead poisoning of the workers themselves is predictable and fairly small. The potential children of workers, however, are not barred from suing, and workers cannot, even if they want to, waive their potential children's right to sue. Clearly, then, the company wants to protect itself against suits by future children with birth defects attributable to genetic or fetal damage for which the company may be found responsible.

But why do they restrict their concern to birth defects transmitted through the mother? There is in our society at the present time, a deeply ingrained indentification of women with reproduction. Thus we tend to think of reproductive hazards only in terms of women—

and of women's occupational health problems only in terms of reproduction. (The first major scientific conference on the occupational health of women workers was almost entirely taken up with such topics as the risks of toxic substances on future generations, birth defects, miscarriages, reproductive dangers, and pregnancy (Stellman, 1977, 81).) This identification gives rise to the "myth of perpetual pregnancy" (Stellman, 1977, 179) according to which any fertile woman is presumed pregnant until proven otherwise. Thus women are not thought of as able to choose whether or not to become pregnant or to continue an unplanned pregnancy. And this makes it seem reasonable and right that they not be permitted to choose whether or not to continue working at a job involving reproductive risks. This attitude helps to explain why the company's policy seems to acknowledge the possible teratogenic (fetal damage) but not mutagenic (genetic damage) effects of lead, since teratogens act only through the female. This emphasis is most convenient for the company, too, since acknowledging mutagenic risks would not allow the appearance that the problem could be dealt with simply by excluding certain people rather than cleaning up the entire operation. Finally, at least one source suggests that a birth defect resulting from maternal exposure would be easier to establish in court than one resulting from paternal exposure.[9] It is not clear to me why this should be the case (unless it is because the attitudes we have been discussing would also influence judges and juries), but the company may, rightly or wrongly, believe it to be. Hence, Cyanamid's policy seems to me to be the result of a desire to protect itself from expensive law suits combined with a stereotypic, discriminatory attitude toward women, rather than from any genuine concern over the welfare of the women or their potential children.

None of this is completely decisive, in my view, as to whether or not paternalism, in Dworkin's sense, is involved in the present case. It has not been my purpose to establish that it is or is not, but to raise and begin to explore considerations relevant to the question so that we may see how issues of paternalism, protective policies, and discrimination tend to be intertwined in actual cases. Once we are alert to these tendencies we may discover them at work even in cases that initially appear much more clear-cut than this one.

It seems appropriate to distinguish between an act or policy being justified and an agent being justified in so acting. We do generally accept the idea that a person can do the right thing for the wrong reason. Applied to our present case, this would mean distinguishing the question, "Is the sterilization-or-exclusion policy justified?" from the question, "Was the American Cyanamid Corp. justified in adopting the sterilization-or-exclusion policy?" It could be, for example, that the company had no right to impose the policy, but the policy itself is a good one, and some other agency, say OSHA, would be justified in adopting it.

Let us now consider whether a policy of excluding fertile women from jobs involving exposure to reproductive hazards could be a justifiable way of preventing birth defects. Would it, for example, be justifiable for OSHA to promulgate such a policy? Note that, although the Cyanamid case stands out due to the explicit nature of the choice presented—your fertility or your job—any policy specifically excluding fertile women implicitly presents that same choice.

The facts of this particular case are such that the policy cannot be justified regardless of who is responsible for it. It does not eliminate the danger of birth defects, and it allows remaining workers to continue working in an environment that is dangerous to their own health. A more effective and nondiscriminatory approach is available: make the job safe for all workers by reducing the exposure levels. But what if the facts were different, as they may turn out to be in some other cases, and what about women who actually are pregnant, since fetuses may in fact be more vulnerable than adults to toxic substances, especially in the early weeks?

On the more general question first, if dangers really were only to and/or through women, would it be justifiable to bar them from certain workplaces? In general, I claim it would not be justifiable to bar women from workplaces in such cases. To do so would be to accept, or require, blatant discrimination against women. Employers should be required to make workplaces safe for both men and women. This is so for a combination of reasons.

First, there is the matter of the violation of reproductive and privacy rights discussed above. These considerations would apply regardless of what person or agency instituted the policy. Thus, even if they are not decisive, they must be placed in the balance.

Second, women constitute slightly more than half the population of the United States. To treat what is a threat to a substantial portion of the population (it need not be a majority, or even near one) as a special vulnerability, a misfortune and inconvenience for the individuals but not the responsibility or concern of society as a whole, much less of private corporations, is more and more coming to be viewed as unacceptable and unjust.

It might be objected that by barring women, society and/or the corporations would be showing their concern and exercising their responsibility. But the point is that excluding them places the entire burden—cost, inconvenience, possible stigma, etc.—upon those in the threatened group, without even any choice about how that burden shall be borne. Thus it is becoming accepted that public facilities and jobs must be made accessible to those confined to wheelchairs, the blind, etc. This way of thinking is reflected, for example, in the Rehabilitation Act of 1973 and Department of Labor regulations which require that federal contractors and subcontractors take affirmative action, including individualized accommodation if necessary to employ and advance qualified handicapped individuals. Insofar as possible, public facilities, workplaces, and social institutions in general should be made flexible enough to adapt to the diversity within the population, rather than requiring individuals to adapt or be excluded. This seems to me correct as a general rule, and its application to the situations under consideration is clear.

It should be mentioned that this rule is by no means universally accepted.[10] Employers in private industry especially tend to push hard in the other direction. If a certain proportion of workers exposed to a substance get rashes, or asthma, or cancer, or byssinosis (brown lung disease of cotton workers), or berylliosis (beryllium disease), the response of the employers—almost universally as far as I have seen—is to claim that certain individuals are "allergic" or "sensitive" to the substance in question, which is otherwise quite safe. The employee may quit, seek a transfer, or go on suffering continued exposure and deteriorating health. It is her or his problem. Opponents argue that, not only is this approach unfair to those directly affected, but their response to the substances in question should be taken as an indication that the substances are probably harmful to humans generally at the exposure levels involved. Individual sensitivity and reaction to harmful substances naturally vary, and the harmful effects of some substances appear only after some time (e.g., ten to forty years for some carcinogens). Hence, the fact that some workers do not suffer acute symptoms is no indication that they are not being harmed.

This tendency on the part of employers to blame the victims of workplace poisoning may also be seen in the current trend toward genetic screening. (See, for example, Severo, 1980.) The idea here is to identify individuals who may be "hypersusceptible" to certain toxic substances because of "defective" genes, and to exclude such persons from jobs in which they would be exposed. Again, opponents view the notions of "hypersusceptibility" and "defective" genes as a misleading and biased description of normal human variation. A person's right to employment, and to a safe and healthful workplace should not be contingent upon the person's having "good" genes. Exclusionary policies, whether based on sex, race, genes or whatever, violate workers' rights because they discriminate against certain groups of workers (or would-be workers) and because they shift the burden of workplace health and safety from company to individual workers. The genetic approach, by the way, reinforces the tendency to focus on sex, race and ethnic origin, due to the relations of race and ethnicity to gene pools and of sex to sex-linked traits. With exclusionary policies, those who remain on the job are very likely not adequately protected, while those who are excluded are "protected" out of a job. As we shall see again and again, if a worker's access to and retention of a job is not reasonably secure, most other protections are empty. It is a cruel and all too frequent irony, then, when those other protections become the pretext for denying a worker a job.

Finally, in addition to the general objections against exclusionary policies, the history and continued practice of discrimination against women makes barring them even more objectionable than it might otherwise be. A point which was passed over earlier is relevant here. The employers' argument, summarized above, ends with the point that the number of women affected by exclusionary policies is negligible, since few women are employed in the industries in question. Since this fact is the result of past discrimination, it should count against, not for, additional discriminatory measures. Moreover, general acceptance of the practice of excluding fertile women from jobs involving reproductive hazards could shut them out of some 20 million or more jobs.[11] These factors render highly suspect even temporary acceptance of exclusionary practices while industry finds ways to make the workplace safe for everyone.

On the relation between protective policies and discrimination, it is interesting to note that, while exclusionary policies have been adopted in many of the higher paying, traditionally male jobs, no such policies are applied in the traditional women's jobs where known reproductive hazards abound: operating room personnel (anesthetic gases); x-ray technicians and flight attendants (radiation); beauticians (propellants—now being phased out for environmental reasons, mutagenic and carcinogenic hair dyes); drycleaning (tetrachlorethylene, a mutagen); meatwrapping (polyvinylchloride); and so on (Wright, 1979, 304–5; *WOHRC News*, 1979). Moreover, historically, protective legislation has not applied to women in low-paid women's jobs. Regulations restricting night work and heavy lifting, for example, were not extended to female hospital workers, who continued to work nights and to lift patients and heavy equipment, or to waitresses who also worked nights and lifted heavy trays (Stellman, 1977, 176–77).

For all these reasons, exclusionary policies ought generally to be avoided even where a hazard is known to work only on or through members of one sex. And we ought to be extremely suspicious of claims that it is not technologically possible or economically feasible to make the workplace safe for all. Still, we must recognize that there may be rare cases in which such a claim is true.

For those few instances where the requirement that the workplace be made safe for all workers may be genuinely unworkable, the recently formed Coalition for the Reproductive Rights of Workers (CRROW) has proposed the following guidelines. An exclusionary policy can be justified only if the employer can prove that (a) it has cleaned up the workplace in compliance with OSHA regulations; (b) substantial scientific evidence exists on the effects of the substance in question on both sexes; (c) this evidence shows that the risk is to only one sex or group; (d) no alternative means exist for reducing or eliminating the risk; (e) the company's policy is to displace as few workers as possible, and these workers are assured of the same pay rate and seniority after transfer (*WOHRC News*, 1979, 6). This seems a reasonable approach, keeping the responsibility upon the company and at the same time recognizing that there may be exceptional cases where exclusion is justified.

Some may argue that no exclusion can be justified—that in the above kind of case, what the company should be required to do is to make the job as safe as possible, fully inform members of the group at risk what the dangers are, and let the individuals make the final decision on whether or not to accept the risks. Not allowing the individual to make that choice seems paternalistic.

In light of our earlier discussion, some may wish at this point to distinguish cases where the danger is exclusively or primarily to the worker from cases where actual fetuses and/or potential offspring are threatened. The charge of unjustified paternalism could then be directed quite forcefully against the former sort of case, the argument being that where only their own lives or health are at risk, once they are fully informed of the nature and extent of the risk, surely only they have the right to decide. (Responses pointing to the burden on society should the individual become disabled would presumably be persuasive only to someone willing to forego freedom of choice in many areas where we normally expect it.) The latter cases would be more complex and controversial, but no doubt some would still maintain that only the individual worker should have the final choice.

I have a great deal of sympathy for this position. I am hesitant to endorse it, however, because I fear that such an approach would tend to shift the total burden of responsibility onto the individual worker. That is, (a) companies would maintain that if, after being fully informed of the risks, a worker chose to stay on, then the company should be absolved of all future liability. (b) Companies would tend to use this "voluntary" approach rather than clean up the workplace, whereas, in order to institute an exclusionary policy they would have to show that they already had cleaned up, at least enough to meet OSHA's standards. While I am not optimistic about enforcement in either case, it seems likely that there would be better and stricter enforcement in the latter one. (c) Companies would be less likely to provide genuinely acceptable alternatives to workers already employed in a risk area. Workers transferred out of a risk area under an exclusionary policy would have to be provided alternative employment at no loss in pay or seniority, according to the CRROW proposal outlined earlier. Would a similar requirement be applicable and enforceable for individual workers who "chose" to leave a risk area?

The words "voluntary" and "chose" appear in scare quotes. This is because whether or not a decision is a voluntary choice depends at least sometimes on what the available alternatives are. And I fear that where matters are left up to individual arrangements between employer and employee, the alternatives will be to choose to stay on and continue to be exposed—at your own risk—or quit.

So I am inclined to think that a very strictly enforced set of restrictions and requirements on exclusionary policies might be preferable to the individual choice approach. Insofar as this is needed— not to protect the workers from themselves, but to prevent the kind of slippage in the burden of responsibility described above—it would not be paternalistic. Still, there is a serious question whether the requirement that all possible alternatives such as additional clean-up beyond OSHA standards, changing production processes, and substitution of less hazardous substances be preferred to exclusion would be genuinely enforceable. Thus, it might be best in the end to bar both the individual choice approach and the exclusionary one and simply require that employers find ways to make workplaces safe.

In cases where a woman is actually pregnant and there is reason to believe that the fetus is at risk, similar considerations apply. Certainly, she should be guaranteed the opportunity for a temporary transfer or leave if no safe work is available out of the area of exposure, with no loss in pay or seniority and the right to return to her original job after the danger is past. Ideally, perhaps, she should be free, given these conditions, to make whatever individual arrangements are, in her judgment, best suited to her particular situation. Here again, though, I would be hesitant to leave these arrangements to be worked out on a "voluntary" individual basis between employer and employee. This is not because the employee might not make the rational or the right decision, but because she might be placed at an extreme disadvantage.

To sum up, then, exclusionary policies are generally unjustifiable at least under existing social conditions. They *may* be justifiable in extremely rare cases, but only if properly restricted. If, in those rare cases, the policies serve to prevent employers from abusing workers' individual vulnerability, they would not be paternalistic. But primary emphasis should be placed on making workplaces safe for everyone, and if even restricted exclusionary policies would undermine this goal, then they are not justifiable at all. Temporary transfers or leaves with pay-rate and seniority retention should, of course, be made available to pregnant women in all jobs where the fetus might be endangered.

Update

In the fall of 1979, the pigment division, in which the women had been sterilized in order to remain working, was shut down by Cyanamid for economic reasons.

On October 9, 1979, OSHA issued a citation against American Cyanamid charging the company had enacted a "policy which required women employees to be sterilized in order to be eligible to work in those areas of the plant where they would be exposed to certain toxic substances." The agency proposed a $10,000 penalty. (Earlier in the same year the company received several other citations from OSHA, including two for "willful violations" exposing workers to excessively high levels of lead and chromates. Then-OSHA director Eula Bingham said, "The reproductive health of workers, both men and women, is a valid part of OSHA's regulatory concern. No worker must be forced to sacrifice his or her right to conceive children in order to hold a job" (*CLUW News*, Fall, 1979). The company planned to challenge the case "with all the resources at its command" (Severo, 1980, 36).

On April 27, 1981, under the Reagan administration, the Occupational Safety and Health Review Commission dismissed the 1979 OSHA citation saying, "An employee's decision to undergo sterilization in order to gain or retain employment grows out of economic and social factors which operate primarily outside the workplace" (*The Guardian*, July 1, 1981).

The women's union, the Oil, Chemical and Atomic Workers Union (OCAW), which had filed the original complaint against Cyanamid, appealed the dismissal to the Court of Appeals for the District of Columbia. Cyanamid tried to block the appeal, arguing that only OSHA could appeal the Review Commission's decision, that OCAW had no authority to do so. OSHA apparently had no intention of appealing. The appeals court ruled that the union could pursue the case. Cyanamid then petitioned the Supreme Court, asking it to rule that OCAW could not appeal. The Supreme Court refused without comment, so the case will be heard by the Court of Appeals.

Another suit was filed against Cyanamid by thirteen women who were affected by the exclusionary policy—including four of the five sterilized women. The American Civil Liberties Union, representing the women in a class action suit, has charged that Cyanamid's policy violated Title VII of the 1964 Civil Rights Act. This suit is scheduled to go to trial in September 1983.

In a related case, an Olin Corporation policy of dividing jobs into three categories, "restricted," "controlled," and "unrestricted," but applying the categories only to fertile women, was found to constitute a prima facie case of sex discrimination. Fertile women were barred from the "restricted" jobs and were required to sign a special form acknowledging "some risk, although slight" in order to work in the "controlled" jobs. The Federal Court of Appeals for the Fourth Circuit made the ruling in December 1982. The court did find, however, that the employer has a legitimate interest in the safety of a fetus and compared this interest to the employer's interest in the safety of business customers. Courts have found in the past that the latter interest can provide a lawful basis for sex discrimination where the safety of the customer is an overriding business necessity. The case was returned to a lower court for a full hearing on whether the discrimination involved in Olin's policy could be excused as "necessary to the safe and efficient operation of the business" (*WOHRC News*, February/March 1983). Thus, the burden of proof is shifted to the employer, but the issue remains unresolved.

Two

The Case of Occidental Chemical

The Occidental Chemical Corporation case which opens this chapter raises different questions about informed consent from those considered in the last chapter. There the focus was on the consent component; here it is on the information component. In this case, workers were sterilized by exposure to a chemical about which they had not been warned. Discussion of the question whether they can be said to have been sterilized without informed consent leads us to consider, in more general terms, some necessary informational conditions for informed consent to workplace hazards. These conditions comprise what occupational safety and health advocates refer to as "the right to know." We explore some employer arguments against the right to know, and conclude that this issue is inextricably connected to the issue of control of the workplace.

Song of the Canary is a documentary film about the dangers of the American workplace by David Davis and Josh Hanig.

> *Narrator:* Coal miners once took caged canaries into the mines. By collapsing and dying, the tiny birds warned of the presence of deadly gases. Today, workers themselves have become the canaries—for other workers and for society as a whole.

The first half of the film is about chemical workers employed at the Occidental Chemical Company in Lathrop, California. "Oxy" is a subsidiary of Occidental Petroleum, as is Hooker Chemical, now infamous for the Love Canal disaster. Workers are seen in different settings: leaving work, in a bar, at home, at the union hall, playing softball. They discuss and demonstrate some of their health problems: headaches, nausea, nose bleeds, internal hemorrhaging, spots on their bodies. Some wonder why none of them has had any children in several years.

The narrator explains that the filmmakers then arranged sperm counts for seven of the men. All seven were sterile. Follow-up tests showed that twenty out of fifty in the agricultural chemical department were sterile. The cause was DBCP (dibromochlorpropane), a pesticide used against nematode worms that attack common root crops and the roots of grape vines and fruit trees.

> *Worker:* I don't want to overpopulate the world, but I did want to have two children. I feel cheated. They're in business to make money, regardless of my life or Jack's life or anyone else's life.

James Lindley, vice president and western regional director of Oxy, is interviewed.

> *Interviewer:* What was your initial feeling when you first found out that in fact these men were sterile?
> *Lindley:* Shock. We had no idea. I had no idea that we had any kind of process here in our plant operations that could do such a thing to a human being.
> *Interviewer:* But hadn't a study been done by Dow Chemical back in 1961 that indicated DBCP did cause sterility in rats?
> *Lindley:* Well, there was a study funded by Dow—that Torkelson study, Dr. Torkelson, and it did not show sterility in rats. What it showed was that with very high doses of DBCP you could get testicular atrophy, if you will, the shriveling up of the testicles. I've talked to two scientists who are familiar with the work, and they both say, "Heck, we just didn't draw the conclusion that there'd be sterility from the fact that the testicles were shriveling up."

Later he is asked about the company's policy on safety.

> *Lindley:* We feel that it's kind of a sales job. You've got to sell safety, if you will, to people so they believe that it's good for them and it's good for the company and it's good for society. . . . Granted, I'm not in the plant very often, but I think that there are lots of potential hazards in all of society, and you learn to live with them.

Jack Hodges, chief steward of the Oil, Chemical and Atomic Workers' Union local at Oxy, has been mixing chemicals for eleven years. His nose bleeds constantly, and he has been hospitalized three times for internal hemorrhages. (He is the 'Jack' referred to by the other worker quoted above.) Jack is asked why people continue to work at a place like Oxy.

> *Hodges:* A worker has to weigh the bad against the good. It doesn't do any good to get up and run. You need the job, so there's nothing to do except stay and fight. Where else are you going to go?
> *Another Worker:* It has shortened my life span. But right now the main thing in my life is raising my kids, so I keep going back in every day.

Pesticides

Pesticides are chemicals that are intended to kill pests such as insects (insecticides), mites (miticides), weeds and unwanted vegetation (herbicides), fungi (fungicides), and rats and other vermin (rodenticides). They enter the human body in three main ways: absorption through the skin into the blood; ingestion in food, water, dust in the air, on hands, cigarettes, etc.; inhalation of dusts and vapors.

Many pesticides are highly stable and accumulate in the food chain at levels often more than a million times greater than those in the general environment. For example, in 1972, about half of the chub and trout caught in Lake Michigan were seized by the Food and Drug Administration (FDA) because they were found to contain residues of aldrin and dieldrin above the permissible levels of 0.3 parts per million. This was a surprise to many since the levels in Lake Michigan's water were in the parts per trillion range. The fact that these chemicals are fat soluble and highly persistent allowed them to accumulate in the food chain at levels nearly a billion times greater than those of the lake water (Epstein, 1979, 253).

There are many different types of pesticides and their effects on humans depend upon the type involved as well as on the intensity and duration of exposure. All are dangerous. Besides sterility, birth defects and cancer, their effects include disorders of the nervous system, headache, weakness, dizziness, blurred vision, sweating, nausea and vomiting, stomach cramps, diarrhea, trouble walking and maintaining balance, difficulty breathing, muscle twitching, fainting, seizures, coma, tremors, chloracne (a persistent and disfiguring skin condition), kidney, liver and bone marrow damage, slowed heartbeat, rapid heartbeat, bleeding lungs and death (LOHP Pesticide Fact Sheet, 1979).

Obviously, everyone is at risk from pesticides through food, water, and general environmental exposure. At most acute risk, however, are workers involved in the production of these substances and agricultural field workers. The latter work in fields that are sprayed with pesticides and irrigated with pesticide-treated water. Not infrequently they are sprayed directly while working in the fields. Rubber boots and gloves are often recommended to help protect against skin absorption. Unless one knows just what chemicals are being used and what their properties are, however, exposure may be increased by the boots and gloves, since some pesticides are absorbed by rubber.[1]

A study conducted at the Johns Hopkins School for Hygiene and Public Health revealed "a marked tendency for more children with brain tumors to have had exposures to insecticides when compared with normal children," and the Environmental Protection Agency has warned that ten and eleven year olds are "likely to be more susceptible to toxic effects of pesticides than adults" (LOHP *Monitor*, Vol. 7, No. 3, May–June 1979, 3).

Discussion

Let us note briefly a few issues that arise in connection with the facts on pesticides just given.

The Fair Labor Standards Act of 1938 outlaws the use of children under age sixteen in industrial labor but permits their employment in agriculture. According to this law, children of twelve years and older may work in agriculture at eighty-five percent of the federal minimum wage. They may not work during school hours, but there are no restrictions on the number of hours per day they may work. Amendments to the Act passed in 1977 authorize the Department of Labor to grant waivers permitting the employment of ten and eleven year-olds as handharvesters of short season crops, but the waivers have been temporarily halted by an injunction obtained by the National Association of Farmworkers Organizations (*WOHRC News*, July/August 1980). The United Farm Workers' Union maintains that children under sixteen should not be employed in agricultural work at all. Adults' wages should be made adequate for the support of their families, and the only way to achieve this is to bar the employment of children in agriculture as in other industries.

In addition to the immediate issue of the potentially greater risk to children of pesticide exposure, more general isues of equal protection are raised here. Agricultural workers are not covered by some OSHA standards, despite the fact that farm labor follows mining and construction as the third most dangerous occupation in this country (*Economic Notes*, Vol. 47, No. 4-5, April–May 1979, 5). And child labor laws do not apply to farm work as they do to labor in other industries. Moreover, exploitation of child labor is permitted in the form of paying less than minimum wage, which also works to limit jobs and depress wages of adult farm workers. The government has estimated that 90 percent of all workers employed in the 1978 strawberry harvest were under sixteen years of age (LOHP *Monitor*, Vol. 7, No. 3, May–June 1979, 3). Agricultural workers are routinely excluded from many of the rights and protections afforded other workers in the United States.

A related set of issues arises in connection with another pesticide, the herbicide Agent Orange. Used as a defoliant by the United States during the war in Vietnam, Agent Orange contained dioxin,[2] which can cause a wide range of health problems ranging from chloracne to cancer, miscarriages and birth defects. Many American soldiers (as well, of course, as Vietnamese soldiers and civilians, and Australian soldiers) were exposed to Agent Orange: those who sprayed it, those who were sprayed with it, and those who entered defoliated areas shortly after spraying. Many Vietnam veterans now suffer serious health problems and/or have fathered children with birth defects which they attribute to Agent Orange exposure. The United States government and the chemical companies which produced Agent Orange have refused to accept responsibility for these problems. Members of the armed forces are employees; yet they lack many of the legal rights and protections of other workers and many of the civil rights of citizens generally.[3]

If the various rights that these workers (farm workers, members of the armed forces, and government employees generally) do not share are moral as well as legal rights of the workers who do enjoy them, then the legal rights ought morally to be extended to the excluded workers unless it can be shown that (a) the excluded workers do not share the moral rights e.g., because features of the situation giving rise to the moral right for most workers are absent from their situations, or (b) factors are present in their situation, but not in that of most workers, which morally justify overriding the moral right in their case. I would argue that most, if not all, of them are moral rights. Certainly health and safety rights, associated reproductive rights, rights against child labor and exploitation, as well as many of the civil rights related to freedom of speech, expression and association that are denied members of the armed forces should be acknowledged as moral rights. And even if some of the legal rights do not themselves reflect or derive from moral rights, a general requirement of justice that may be formulated as a moral right to equal treatment for persons in circumstances that are alike in relevant ways would require that some moral justification be provided for excluding some workers.

That farm work, unlike industrial work, is good, healthy, outdoor work, which is good for children and does not pose health and safety threats to workers generally, may once have been plausible. In view of the prevalence of pesticides and more and bigger machinery, the health problems now known to be associated with stoop labor, and the status of agricultural work as the third most dangerous in the nation, it is not plausible today. And national security ought to be scrutinized very carefully as a justification for the wholesale denial of civil and employee rights to members of the armed forces.

Most directly related to the primary concerns of the remainder of the present discussion are the following interrelated issues: (a) the reproductive effects of exposure to pesticides (including that of children whose reproductive systems are still in the process of development); (b) the facts that farm workers and Vietnam veterans are and were exposed to these and other hazards without being informed of the nature or magnitude of the risks involved; and (c) the question of satisfaction of a requirement of informed consent to exposure to serious reproductive and other health hazards. The issue of informed consent raises especially serious problems in relation to child workers on the one hand and draftees on the other.[4] Let us now explore these three issues in relation to the case presented at the opening of this chapter.

There are obvious similarities and differences between the American Cyanamid case of the preceding chapter and the Occidental Chemical case. One difference—that the former case involves the sterilization of women while the latter involves the sterilization of men—is worth noting just for its value as a concrete illustration of the fact that reproductive rights and hazards are not only women's problems. The effects of Agent Orange on the new generation promise to be a grim reminder of this fact.

The notion of informed consent connects the two main topics of our present discussion: As applied to sterilization and exposure to reproductive hazards, it ties in with our concern about reproductive rights. Its specific application in the Oxy case introduces the general issue of workers' right to know about hazards they are exposed to in the workplace. In the last chapter I argued that, because the company's offer to allow the women to keep their jobs if they had themselves sterilized was substantially coercive, the consent of the women to be sterilized was not fully genuine. Thus they could be said to have been sterilized without informed consent. Can the same be said of the Oxy case?

In the Oxy case, there could not, of course, be informed consent because the workers were not informed that DBCP would or could sterilize them.[5] Still, it seems odd to call this a case of *sterilization* without informed consent. I can think of two reasons for this: sterilization was not part of the end or goal of any person or the purpose of any action involved, and sterilization was not a certain (or foreseen) outcome of working with DBCP. Let us consider these in turn.

1. Sterilization was not part of the end or goal of any person or the purpose of any action involved. This point could be meant in one or both of two distinct, though possibly related, ways. I shall call them the terminological point and the substantive point for easy reference.

The terminological point is that it seems linguistically incorrect and misleading to speak of the *sterilization* of a person when achieving his or her sterility was not the intent of any of the persons involved. On this way of hearing the word "sterilization," it seems to function analogously to the word "execution."[6] An execution cannot properly be said to have taken place unless someone intentionally carried it out. But "sterilization" need not have that implication. Grammatically, sterility is the state of being sterile, and sterilization is a process or event leading to sterility, intended or not, foreseen or not. "Sterilization"is more like "fertilization" than like "execution" in this respect.[7] If I go out to my garden with a small paint brush and carefully lift pollen from the male squash blossoms and deposit it in the female blossoms, I fertilize those blossoms. Fortunately, however, the ants and the bees do the job just as well without intending to. Fertilization takes place either way.

This brings us to the substantive point which may be put as follows: When "sterilization" is used in such a way as not to imply intent, then it makes no sense to ask about sterilization without informed consent. We have not yet dealt with the question of whether, or to what extent, sterilization was or should have been, *foreseen* as a consequence of exposure to DBCP. But in order to respond to the present point, we must distinguish between outcomes that are *intended* and outcomes that are *foreseen* but *not intended*. For it might make no sense to ask about informed consent to an outcome that was not, and could not have been, foreseen, and still make perfectly good sense to ask about informed consent to an outcome that was (or should have been) foreseen, even though it was not intended.

How much difference does it make whether sterilization is the intended purpose of a procedure or a predictable though unintended outcome? To show that there is a morally significant difference between bringing about a particular outcome as part of the point or purpose of one's action, and bringing it about as a foreseen but unintended consequence, one would have to invoke something like the Catholic principle of double effect.

According to this principle, certain acts are permissible which will bring about, as a foreseen but unintended consequence, an effect which, were it intended—either as the end of the act or as a means to the end—would render the act impermissible. For example, it is permissible to remove the cancerous womb of a pregnant woman in order to save her life, even though, in so doing, one removes the fetus with the womb and brings about the death of the fetus. It is not permissible, on the other hand, to inject a saline solution into the womb to detach the fetus from the uterine wall in order to end a pregnancy which, if continued, will cost the pregnant woman's life. The reason is that the way in which the saline solution causes the fetus to detach is by killing the fetus. Thus the death of the fetus is a means to the end of saving the woman's life, so the act is not permitted.

Now this principle is controversial at best. There are those who deny that there is any morally significant difference between those consequences of an act that an agent intends and those that he or she foresees but does not intend. Others are sympathetic to the idea that there is *sometimes* a morally significant difference, but they may not agree among themselves about which times. The idea here seems to be that there are certain kinds of acts that may themselves never be done, such as directly and intentionally killing an innocent person; yet it may, in some circumstances, be permissible to do another kind of act, not bad in itself, and undertaken for an extremely important reason, which will have as an unavoidable consequence, the death of an innocent person. An example cited in a recent article is "the killing of noncombatants in a justified military action . . . : the action may be justified—even if it is foreseen that some noncombatants will certainly be killed—if killing them is not a means of achieving one's military objective, since in this case undertaking the action may be presumed to be in itself good, the bringing about of the deaths is not intended, and there is a grave reason for the action" (Boyle, 1980, 528–29).

Here is another example: Suppose you believe, as many Catholics and others do, that intentionally having oneself sterilized is morally impermissible. Keeping one's job is in itself permissible, or even a good thing to do; and supporting one's family is a grave reason for keeping one's job. According to the principle of double effect, it would be impermissible for the women at Cyanamid to have themselves sterilized as a means to keeping their jobs. But the men at Oxy, even if—contrary to actual fact—they knew all along that they would become sterile, would have done nothing impermissible in accepting sterility as the price of keeping their jobs. This seems to me a distinction without a difference.[8]

Even if the principle of double effect is accepted, though, it does not help establish that the Oxy case does not involve sterilization without informed consent. For, to return to the abortion example, supposing it is permissible to remove the cancerous womb of a pregnant woman, it surely is not permissible to do so without ensuring that she understands that this will bring about the death of the fetus (assuming, of course, that she is not in a coma, etc.). Similarly, even if unintended but foreseen sterilization sometimes has a different moral status from intended sterilization, this in no way diminishes the right of the person affected to be informed that sterilization will or may result before deciding whether or not to proceed. Thus even if the principle of double effect is accepted, unintended but foreseen sterilization of workers wihout their knowledge ought to count as sterilization without informed consent: a serious violation of reproduction rights. Whatever is justified in the intuition that the Oxy case is not one of sterilization without informed consent must, it seems, rest on point (2).

2. Sterilization was not a certain or foreseen outcome of working with DBCP.

As we have seen the notion of informed consent involves two components: the informational component, with which we are concerned in this chapter, and the consent component, which we considered in Chapter One. Obtaining informed consent is a requirement that must normally be satisfied before one person (or agency) may justifiably do certain sorts of things to or for another, or subject another to certain sorts of experiences, procedures, or risks. Thus this notion involves two parties: the person *giving* informed consent and the person or agency *obtaining* it. Where a requirement of informed consent is invoked, it is normally proper to make the following two assumptions: (a) there is a person or agency to whom the requirement applies, i.e., the party required to *obtain* informed consent; and (b) that party has (or ought to have) the information which, if communicated to the potentially affected person, would constitute satisfaction of the informational component of the requirement.

Point (2), then, may be seen as arguing that this second assumption was not satisfied, and hence it is inappropriate to invoke the notion of informed consent, as one does in claiming that the Oxy workers were sterilized without informed consent.

In our present case, we can identify the employer, Occidental Chemical, as the agency, and responsible Oxy officials as the persons to whom the requirement, if applicable, applies. There is a wide range of possibilities concerning the state of Oxy officials' knowledge or belief during the time the workers were exposed to DBCP. Here is a sampling:

i. It is certain that all exposed workers will become sterile. Risk to any given worker of becoming sterile due to exposure $= 1$.

ii. It is highly probable that all or most exposed workers will become sterile or have reduced sperm counts. Risk to any given worker of sterilization or reduced sperm count due to exposure is very high.

iii. It is virtually certain that some exposed workers will become sterile and some will have reduced sperm counts. Risk to any given worker of becoming sterile due to exposure $= .n$; of reduced sperm count due to exposure $= .m$.

iv. It is highly probable that some workers will become sterile and some will have reduced sperm count, but the precise risk to any given worker is unknown (insufficient data).

v. There is reason to believe that there is some risk to fertility and/or other reproductive function of exposed workers.

vi. There is reason to believe that there may be some risk to fertility and/or other reproductive function of exposed workers.

vii. There is no reason to believe that there is any risk to fertility or other reproductive function of exposed workers.

Now it appears, based on subsequent investigations, that the actual situation was something like (ii) or (iii), with the m and n numbers fairly high.[10] But what we must ask are two other questions: what the Oxy officials knew or believed at the time, and what they should reasonably have known or believed at the time.

It seems likely that the actual beliefs of the Oxy officials were one or more of (iv) through (vii). It is possible that none of them actually believed (iv), or perhaps even (v). Indeed, it is possible, though not at all probable, that they all believed (vii).

Now, while the requirements concerning informed consent will no doubt vary widely over the range (i)–(vii), it seems to me that the only case in which the question of informed consent does not arise at all is (vii). And I would add, not merely where (vii) is actually believed, but where it is known or reasonably believed. That is, even if some or all of the Oxy officials actually believed (vii) they may still have failed to satisfy the requirements of informed consent if they *should reasonably* have known or believed something else.

While there undoubtedly are cases where workers are exposed to risks that the employer has no way of knowing about and no reason to believe exist, and it may be true that in such cases the workers' rights are not violated, I would argue that the Oxy case is not one of them. To say that "we just didn't draw the conclusion that there'd be sterility from the fact that the testicles were shriveling up," does not absolve the company of responsibility. They should at least have considered the possibility of a connection—and that would have taken them at least to belief (vi). Again, for officials to say that they were not aware of the Torkelson study until after the sperm tests does not get them off the hook. In the first place, it is hardly credible that responsible officials of a major chemical company would be unaware of the relevant research. And, in the second place, even if they were not aware of it, they should have been. Rights can be violated by negligence. So, if the Oxy officials believed (vii), the workers' rights may have been violated by the employer's negligence in not keeping up with the relevant research or in not considering an obvious and reasonable inference.

Moreover, I suggest that, since general knowledge about the dangers of pesticides should have been sufficient for belief of (vi) (There is reason to believe that there *may be* some risk . . .), the additional information provided by the Torkelson study, combined with that general knowledge, should have sufficed for belief of (v) (There is reason to believe that there *is* some risk . . .). So I am suggesting that Oxy officials should reasonably have believed at least (v) rather than (vi) or (vii), since they should reasonably have known of the Torkelson study and have considered its implications.

Now consider the following:

1. An employer knows or believes, or ought reasonably to know or believe, that there is reason to believe that there is some risk to the fertility (and/or other reproductive functions) of employees from exposure to a substance on the job.
2. The employer does not inform the employees of this potential risk, thus depriving them of the opportunity to take it into account in major plans and decisions concerning employment and family.
3. Some of the workers become sterile as a result of exposure to the substance in question.

Is it appropriate, in such a case, to say that the employees mentioned in (3) were sterilized without informed consent? To be sure, this is not one of the "standard" or clear-cut instances, but that *may* be the only reason why some people remain reluctant to call it an instance of sterilization without informed consent. Our purpose here is not so much to fit the facts squarely into ready categories, but to see how the categories apply or are relevant to the facts. While "central" or clear-cut instances are useful for clarifying such notions as informed consent, once they are fairly clear we ought to be able to use them in dealing with more complex and difficult ("off-center") cases—which may in turn help to fill out our understanding of these notions.

Due to the uncertainty at the time concerning the results of exposure to DBCP, it may seem more natural to speak of the Oxy case as an instance of occupational exposure to reproductive risks without informed consent—or, more generally still, of occupational exposure to health or safety risks without informed consent. And it is indeed an instance of each of these. Thus we have a basis for the claim that the case involves violation of the reproductive rights of workers, as well as of their general right to know about risks and hazards on the job, even without the claim that it also involves sterilization without informed consent. But note that all of the DBCP workers were exposed to the above risks without informed consent, whether or not their fertility was affected. Those who became sterile were not merely exposed to a risk, they were in fact sterilized, and if they did not give informed consent to the risk, they can hardly have given it to the sterilization.

Treating their cases as cases of sterilization rather than, or in addition to, exposure to risk seems to me useful in that it moves the discussion from the rather abstract and impersonal notions of risk and probability and requires us to consider the actual consequences (whether foreseen, intended or not) for actual individuals. I shall not press this question further here. However one ends up answering it, it seems to me important that it be raised and explored.

In the earlier discussion of reproductive rights, I suggested that they include, among other things, the right to make freely or without coercion one's own decisions about whether and when to have children and at what risk, and about how best to carry out those decisions. We may now add: the right not to have one's capacity to have children, or the children themselves, damaged unnecessarily by preventable occupational (and/or environmental) exposure to reproductive hazards, and the right to be fully informed of potential and/or unpreventable reproductive hazards, and to monitoring of their effects.

Thus reproductive rights overlap with another important cluster of rights, grouped by those involved in efforts to secure them under the general heading of "the right to know."

The right-to-know issue has four essential components, briefly referred to as labeling, posting, personal medical records, and monitoring records. They may be spelled out as follows:

1. The right to know what substances one is working with. In practice, this means the labeling of containers with generic names of potentially harmful substances they contain, along with appropriate warnings, emergency procedures, etc.
2. The right to know the specific dangers involved in one's work and how to protect oneself. In practice, this means (a) the prominent posting in hazardous work areas of warnings indicating the nature of the hazard, recommended precautions, symptoms of acute and chronic poisoning, and emergency procedures, and (b) adequate education and training of workers in dangerous jobs.
3. The right of access to one's personal medical records compiled and maintained by the employer.
4. The right of access to general employer health and safety records, e.g., accident and illness statistics, exposure monitoring data involving both workplace monitoring, such as air sample data, and worker monitoring, such as chest x-rays and levels of lead or other substances in the blood.

It may seem natural to suppose that labeling requirements for toxic substances would be at least as stringent for industrial as for consumer uses. Industrial workers are subject to far more intense, prolonged and repeated exposure than most consumers, day after day, often for twenty or thirty years. That they should have knowledge of what they are being exposed to, and of the relevant precautions and emergency procedures, seems a matter of such obvious common sense that one may tend to assume that, with a very few exceptions, provision of such information would be routine. Workers should not have to fight for information so essential to their health and survival.

In fact, however, many substances used in American workplaces are known to their purchasers and users only by a tradename or code number. A container may have no other identification of the substance inside, except, perhaps for a "Flammable" warning required by the Department of Transportation, or something about corrosive properties or lead content. In a booklet published by the American Lung Association, J. Marion Anderson reports on a study conducted by the National Institute for Occupational Safety and Health:

> NIOSH conducted a national occupational hazards survey of 5,200 workplaces in an attempt to determine the extent of the trade-name problem. In 70 percent of the instances in which they found a person exposed to a potential hazard, the hazard was known only by a trade

name or code number. In 90 percent of those cases, NIOSH could not determine the contents of the trade-name substances either from the container or from information available at the plant. In short, neither employers nor employees knew what substances people were being exposed to, much less their toxic effects.

Seeking more detailed information, NIOSH asked the manufacturers of the mystery trade-name substances for a list of ingredients. The investigators learned that 45 percent of the products in question contained substances supposedly regulated by OSHA because of their recognized toxic potential. About 30 percent of the products contained another trade-name product purchased from a different manufacturer, with the complete contents of the final product known to no one. And, most disturbing of all, 427 different trade-name products encountered in the survey contained one of the 15 carcinogens (cancer-producing agents) that are supposed to be strictly regulated by OSHA. Neither the buyers nor the handlers of the products knew about the carcinogens. [Anderson, 1979, 77–78]

In January 1981, OSHA proposed a labeling standard that would provide for precise chemical identification and appropriate warnings on containers of hazardous substances. Then-director of OSHA Eula Bingham said, in announcing the proposal, "Workers have a right to know what substances they work with on the job, and today many of them don't. Workers who know what they are working with and what the hazards of these substances are will be more likely to take the necessary precautions to safeguard their health. If they develop health problems . . . they will have concrete information to give their personal physicians" (quoted in LOHP *Monitor*, Vol. 9, No. 2, March–April 1981, 10). However, the proposed standard has been "withdrawn indefinitely" by President Reagan's Secretary of Labor, Raymond Donovan.

With regard to the specific dangers involved in the actual work process, neither posting of warnings nor adequate training in the use of hazardous substances or the operation of machinery is common. There are posting requirements included in the OSHA standards for exposure to asbestos and a few other carcinogens, but otherwise posting is virtually unheard of. Of course, as long as substances are not labeled, the usefulness of posting would be undermined to some degree by workers being unable to identify the substances they were being warned about.

Instead of informative posting that warns of specific hazards and details precautionary and emergency procedures, workers most often get the ubiquitous "Safety First," "Work Safely," and "People Cause Accidents" signs that insult their intelligence and blame them for accidents. Instead of serious training in health and safety on the job, they get corporate safety campaigns in which teams compete for prizes for the longest period without a lost-time accident. The Sheraton Hotel's "Safe Way Program," for example, includes an employee handbook that "explains" that 85 percent of work injuries are due to unsafe behavior while only 15 percent are due to unsafe conditions. In addition, it includes a "Safe Team" competition in which teams of two hundred workers compete for the chance to participate in a drawing for a color television set or a car, for thirty or ninety days, respectively, without a lost-time accident *(Sheraton World,* August 1979).

A lost-time accident is one in which the injured worker misses one or more full days of work. Lost-time data are used by the Bureau of Labor Statistics, National Safety Council, legislators and lobbyists, insurance underwriters and the National Association of Manufacturers (which uses them to claim that "the average American is safer in the workplace than at home"). In many states employers' premiums for workers' compensation insurance are based on lost-time data. Employers thus have a serious interest in keeping their lost-time figures down—whatever the actual number and severity of accidents suffered—and have devised many ways to do so. An injured worker will be urged to report to work on the next scheduled workday, even if unable to work for several days or weeks. The worker often goes along rather than lose wages, which are at best only partly replaced by workers' compensation. If the worker is unable to report to work, he or she may be encouraged to take vacation or sick days, which do not count as lost time. Workers are offered informal cash settlements for their injuries so that they will not file a claim for workers' compensation. If no claim is filed, there is no independent check on the employer's data, so the accident can go unreported. The cash settlement is usually less than they would get in compensation, but they know that if they file, the claim may be denied, and even if approved it may take months or years to collect. So they "voluntarily" settle for cash in hand.

Even if properly observed, the lost-time standard would fail to record some 90 percent of injuries that are serious but not disabling, involving, for example, eye injuries, loss of consciousness, fractures, restriction of work or motion, or assignment to another job because of an injury. Such injuries would be recorded only in those cases where at least a full day's work was lost.

Safety competitions are another device to keep lost-time numbers low. Workers are discouraged from reporting accidents and staying out of work by their desire not to ruin the team's record. Thus, rather than preventing accidents, these schemes result in accidents going unreported and injured workers untreated.[11]

We see here one of many direct links between different aspects of the right-to-know issue: adequate posting and training in health and safety *versus* blaming the victim and "safety" competitions on the one hand, and access to, and accuracy of, monitoring data, specifically accident records, *versus* recording only lost-time accidents, with emphasis on keeping the numbers as low as possible, on the other.

Another reason why employers are reluctant to undertake informative labeling and posting is the fear that any acknowledgment that a substance or work process is hazardous will result in the employer being held liable in case of disease, injury, or death. Without information about the effects of exposure to various substances, a worker may never connect his or her symptoms (e.g., recurrent cold, constant sore throat, sinusitis, shortness of breath, "run-down" feeling, insomnia, irritability, skin rash, etc.) to his or her job. Thus, this information is needed by workers for protection of their health and safety, for treatment of existing health problems, for making informed decisions about whether and under what conditions to remain in a job that is, or may be, making them sick, and for instructing their collective bargaining representatives regarding their concerns and priorities. But it is against the employers' interests to provide it. Therefore, unless the right of workers to this information is recognized and enforced by law, it is not likely to be respected in practice.

Questions and issues concerning the physician-patient relationship[12] take on added dimensions when the physician and patient are employees of the same employer. The most general and difficult problem seems to be the almost inevitable conflict of interest that will arise for the employee-doctor in his or her relationship to the employer on the one hand and the worker-patient on the other. Assuming that, as a physician, the company doctor's primary duties and responsibilities are to the worker-patient, what is he or she to do about the fact that his or her salary is paid, and terms and conditions of employment set, by the employer? Frequently the only choice is to obey the wishes of the employer or give up one's job.

Similar complications arise for company-employed research scientists whose research subjects are the company's workers. While the primary responsibility of research scientists is not generally taken to be to their subjects, but to the scientific community or perhaps the society as a whole, there exist federally mandated guidelines with fairly strong informed consent requirements for all institutions doing federally funded research on human subjects. But for company-funded workplace research, such guidelines are absent. As Thomas Murray writes,

> In the ethics of occupational health research done within companies we are at roughly the stage of most research with human subjects twenty years ago—dependent on the judgment and integrity of the researcher. Whether or not subjects are asked for their consent, whether or not they are informed of the purposes of the research or even that the research is taking place, whether or not the results of their participation are kept confidential, ultimately rely on the choice of the investigator *or his or her superiors.* [Murray, 1983, 7. Emphasis added.]

The existing guidelines for institutions doing federally funded research on human subjects evolved as it was recognized that reliance on the judgment and integrity of researchers too often resulted in serious unwarranted harm to subjects and other violations of their rights. In the workplace case, even if a researcher's judgment is not impaired by zealous pursuit of new knowledge or publications, his or her integrity may be sorely tried if the employer's concerns differ from the researcher's, as the following example illustrates.

> At Dow Chemical, cytogenetics tests were given to determine whether workers who started with "good genes" suffered undue breakage of chromosomes, or bundles of genes, because of exposure to toxic chemicals. Such breakage is suspected as a harbinger of cancer.
>
> When a Dow geneticist did find evidence of undue chromosome breakage among workers exposed to benzene, a widely used chemical and a known carcinogen, the company refused to inform anyone.
>
> "We wanted them to tell the workers what we had found, reduce the levels of benzene to which workers were exposed and inform the appropriate government agencies and the rest of the petro-chemical industry," the geneticist, Dr. Dange J. Picciano [said]. But Dow refused, saying the data were hard to evaluate and that it would have been irresponsible to alarm workers with evidence that might eventually prove inaccurate. Dr. Picciano and several of his colleagues have left Dow. [*WOHRC News*, April/May 1980]

While it is reasonable to suppose that physicians and research scientists have more employment options than most workers, it is not realistic to expect that most of them will come out on the right side of such a fundamental conflict of interest most of the time.[13]

The primary concerns of corporate medical departments and the implications for workers' access to information as well as for the privacy of the patient-physician relationship are illustrated by the following extract from the *Medical Manual*, an instruction manual for medical department personnel at Standard Oil of Indiana:

Any employee alleging an industrial injury will be asked to fill out, if he has not already done so, a "Report of Accident Form." He will be seen by a company physician, who will, in addition to examining the patient, take a careful history of matters having possible bearing on the complaint; a copy of the medical department report (FORM 53-117) will be sent to the Claims Attorney.

In any questionable case, or in any case in which referral to an outside physician appears to be indicated, the Claims Attorney will be contacted by telephone while the patient is still in the Medical Department. (A typical case would be an alleged back injury where objective findings are lacking.) The Claims Attorney and physician will discuss the case and agree on a course of action. No referrals will be made to an outside physician before contacting the Claims Attorney.

It should be noted that all claims cases are adversary cases, and the comments of company physicians to employees must be guarded as to causation and as to liability for costs. . . .

Because claims cases and absences from work due to real or alleged occupational injuries and illness are a significant cost item for the company, the Medical Department will evaluate such cases critically and frequently as to their ability to return to work, and approve them to do so as soon as possible. Doubtful and disputed cases should be discussed with the Claims Attorney on a regular basis. [Quoted in Berman, 1978, 108–9]

Concerning rights of privacy of one's own medical records, the employee-physician and worker-patient situation raises questions of routine management access to workers' medical records. Such access is very widespread according to testimony at hearings on the OSHA standard providing for worker access to these same records. Often higher management, immediate supervisors, personnel staff, and legal staff or counsel have routine access to a worker's medical records without even asking the physician, much less the worker. And company physicians commonly testify without the consent of the employee (and often favorably to the employer's interests) in arbitration and workers' compensation cases (*Federal Register*, Vol. 45, no. 102, May 23, 1980, pp. 35234–37).

Workers are well aware of this, and of the fact that uses of this information that benefit or protect the employer will take priority over uses that benefit or protect the worker—unless the two happen to coincide. The employee may find him or herself "protected" out of a job or into a lower paying or less desirable job if the medical or monitoring record indicates health damage for which the employer may be held liable. *This is the primary reason for the apparently unreasonable reluctance of workers to submit to company medical examinations and monitoring programs.* Where workers object to them, these examinations themselves constitute violations of their right to privacy, in addition to any violation resulting from lack of confidentiality of the records. And, of course, this reluctance, actually very reasonable under the circumstances, is even greater when the workers themselves do not have access to the information, and sometimes are not told what they are being monitored and tested for.

In addition to the right of patients' access to their own medical records, then, their right to privacy of those records and to protection against use of those records to which they do not consent, take on special importance for worker-patients. One possible partial protection against use of a worker's medical records against his or her wishes could be provided by generalizing a suggestion from the last chapter and providing that an employee removed from a work assignment because of actual or potential health damage resulting from that assignment may not be made to suffer loss of pay or seniority as a result. If such a provision were adopted, the question would remain whether or not it was justifiable to *require* a worker to accept a transfer or leave of absence if he or she preferred to remain on the original job. As in the last chapter, I am less confident about this, but I suspect that in practice the problem would arise very rarely if the protection really were adequate.

The more fundamental problems of conflict of interest for company doctors, and non-medically motivated management control of, access to, and potential abuse of workers' personal medical records suggest that an alternative system of occupational medicine is needed, in which the physicians are independent, i.e., neither employees of nor under direct contract to the employer. Such a sytem could be funded and run in any of a variety of ways, but perhaps the most natural and desirable would be as an integral part of a national public health program. We cannot pursue this idea here.

Privacy considerations arise also in that employees frequently are asked or are required to authorize release of their medical records, e.g., to insurance companies, who in turn may release them to the employer's accounting or benefits department. The 1976 Privacy Protection Study Commission found this the most persuasive reason favoring the right of access to one's own medical records:

> So long as it is thought acceptable, or even necessary, for an individual's past or present medical condition to be taken into account in making non-medical decisions about him, he will be asked to allow others to have access to his medical records or at least some of the information in them. As a practical matter, however, his authorization allowing such access to a third party will be meaningless so long as he

does not know and cannot find out, what is in the records. Both theoretically and practically, authorization is a meaningless procedure unless the individual knows what he is authorizing to be disclosed. [Quoted in *Federal Register*, Vol. 45, no. 102, May 23, 1980, p. 35229]

In this way, then, the right of access is a necessary condition for a meaningful right to privacy.

The issue of privacy arises also in connection with workers' access to monitoring records (which involve not only themselves but other workers as well) and with access of unions or other worker representatives to both personal and monitoring records. Clearly workers and their representatives need this information in order to determine, for example, whether a particular health problem an individual experiences is shared by other employees, and whether there are patterns of such problems associated with exposure to certain substances, participation in certain processes, etc. Only in this way can job-related health problems be identified and dealt with. In general, both the right to privacy and the right of access can be satisfied fairly easily in the case of exposure monitoring records by providing the relevant statistical information without personal identification.

Individual and union access to monitoring records that show *effects*, not just exposure levels, and union access to personal medical records present somewhat trickier problems. Exposure levels alone will not help to identify health problems which may be resulting from exposures that, e.g., satisfy the current OSHA standard, but are still damaging to health. Unions have argued that they need this additional information in order adequately to represent their members in collective bargaining. Yet there is some force to the claim that information showing health effects, such as sperm counts, lung function tests, etc., is more private than exposure level data, such as blood lead levels, and hence should be more protected. I am inclined to think that *if* the identities of the individuals can be protected, the importance of the right of access to the information should override any remaining privacy interest in preventing disclosure even in anonymous form.

Union access to personal medical records presents the following dilemma: These records might turn up health problems that would not show up in monitoring records because workers are not being monitored or tested for them—problems that workers consult the company physician about on their own. And they may turn up combinations of symptoms or problems which will point to a particular cause that would not be identifiable from statistical data that do not show whether the same or different workers are exposed to various substances or are experiencing various problems. On the other hand, individual workers might object to a union having access to their personal medical records, whether out of a sense of privacy alone, or out of fear that the information may be misused. Whatever the reason, it seems that this objection ought to be respected. One possibility might be to provide workers with—and clearly inform them of—the following options: a) explicit consent gives union access to individual's record (with or without name as specified by the worker); b) explicit denial of consent gives union no access to record; c) absence of explicit consent or denial is interpreted as tacit consent to union access without name.

We should note two additional areas of concern, which are relevant to the right to know. One is control and/or suppression of relevant research by corporate and industry interests. The other is the almost complete lack of education of doctors and other medical personnel in occupational medicine.

Typically, the relevant research takes place under one (or more) of the following rubrics: (a) government-sponsored and/or conducted research—often dominated by industry-connected "experts"; (b) university-based research—sometimes directly commissioned by, almost always directly or indirectly supported by, corporate funds; (c) research carried out by the corporations themselves in their own laboratories and workplaces; (d) research conducted in independent laboratories under direct commission and control of corporations or industry groups; (e) research conducted and/or commissioned by unions or other worker groups or representatives; (f) research conducted by completely independent researchers. Clearly corporate/industry interests are frequently in a position to influence the direction and the reporting (or non-reporting) of research in the first four categories. And they do (see, for example, Brodeur, 1974, 146ff, 178–79, 198ff, 216–38; Epstein, 1979, 92–95; Bosch, 1978, 51–65; and Scott, 1974, 29, 68–72). In addition, employers frequently refuse to cooperate with research in the fifth and sixth categories, denying researchers access to their premises and to information on substances being used, as well as to monitoring records and lists of previous employees (for researchers trying to do follow-up studies to determine long-term effects of exposures (see, for example, Brodeur, 1974, 8–9). Obviously, if information about the toxic effects of a substance is never ascertained due to corporate control of the direction of research (and refusal to cooperate with research beyond its control) or is suppressed because it is perceived as threatening to corporate/industry interests, it will not be available for labeling or posting even if these rights are recognized. On the other hand, if workers and unions have access to information in all four aspects of the right to know, this can be made available to union and independent researchers.

The lack of education of doctors and other medical personnel in occupational medicine is startling—after all, the great majority of people spend half or more of their waking lives at their work. What they do and are exposed to during all this time might be expected to be of more than a little relevance to their health and to the identification, diagnosis and treatment of health problems. Yet doctors generally are not taught about occupational disease in medical school, are not trained to recognize it, or even to look for it; they virtually never take occupational histories, for example, and seldom ask for the details of a patient's job (Berman, 1978, 94–102). Moreover, doctors and hospitals often have a direct interest in not pursuing occupational causes of disease. If an illness is job-related, Blue Cross-Blue Shield will not pay for treatment. Hence, lung disease gets diagnosed and treated simply as pulmonary fibrosis without pursuing the nature of the fibrosis (asbestosis, byssinosis, sylicosis, etc.).

Some consequences of this practice are, first, the individual may still be working with the harmful substance, unwittingly making the problem worse, rather than separating him or herself from the source of the problem. Second, if the disease is or becomes disabling, the person will not be in a position to collect compensation because he or she does not know it is occupationally related. Third, the employer, not identified as responsible in any way, does nothing to reduce or eliminate the hazard, so others continue to be exposed and will become diseased. And fourth, the magnitude of the problem of occupational disease in general, and of the dangers of the particular substance involved, are grossly underestimated. To illustrate this last point, a survey by the National Institute for Occupational Safety and Health (NIOSH) showed that, of over 900 persons examined, 28 percent had some occupational disease. Fewer than 10 percent of these had been recorded in official documents as required by law. Thus, over 90 percent of occupational diseases were officially unrecognized (Anderson, 1979, 3).

Another consequence of the general lack of education in occupational medicine is that the practice of it is left almost exclusively to company doctors whose primary loyalty, as we have seen, must be to the companies that pay their salaries if they are to keep their jobs. Thus workers often get no information, or they get misinformation, about their condition.

There are two main arguments manufacturers/employers give

against all four aspects of the workers' right to know (labeling containers, posting worksites with generic names of substances and hazard warnings, access to personal medical records, and access to monitoring records). The first is the trade-secret argument. Manufacturers claim that if such information were provided trade secrets might be divulged. Thus, they maintain that the information is private property which they cannot be required to reveal, since it is of such a nature that its value depends on its remaining undisclosed. It is debatable whether withholding this information from workers effectively protects trade secrets in this time of sophisticated chemical analysis. What is certain is that it effectively prevents workers from knowing what hazards they are exposed to, and hence from taking steps and making decisions crucial to their lives and well-being. And even if it is the case that the identity of a chemical could be a trade secret, as in the case of secret catalysts and intermediates that could not be discovered by chemical analysis of the end product, it is difficult to see how anyone could seriously claim that the property right in a trade secret takes precedence over the right to know the nature and effects of hazards one is exposed to in one's work. This is especially so considering the central importance of this latter right to the survival, health, and self-determination of the exposed individuals.[14]

Moreover, as witnesses at hearings on the OSHA standard for access to personal medical records and exposure records pointed out, even where access to this information might reveal trade secrets previously unknown to workers, there is no reason to expect that information would be abused. In the first place, workers have access to trade secret information in the normal course of their jobs, and are routinely required to sign pledges of confidentiality. No evidence was introduced showing either isolated instances or a history of abuse of that information. No reason was given to expect the situation to be different with any new information that the right to know might provide them. Moreover, the scope of trade secret information available to workers is far more limited than that available to management personnel, and again, there is no reason to believe that the potential for abuse by workers is any greater than for abuse by individuals in management. Finally, it was pointed out that workers and their unions generally have an interest in protecting trade secrets in order to protect their jobs (*Federal Register*, Vol. 45, no. 102, May 23, 1980, pp. 35237–39).

The second argument employers give against the right to know is that if workers are given too much information about the hazards they are exposed to or about their own medical condition they will not understand the information correctly, misinterpret the information, and/or become unduly alarmed.

To a large extent these are familiar arguments for the view that physicians have a right or duty to withhold certain kinds of information from patients. I cannot go into all of these general arguments here. The current trend, both in theory and in practice, is away from this view and toward the view that the patient has a right to all information concerning his or her condition, and the physician has a duty, in the absence of explicit authorization by the patient to withhold certain kinds of information, to provide all information. If a patient is to make crucial decisions about and participate actively in his or her treatment, as each one has a right to do, he or she must have all the relevant information. And if a patient's condition is terminal, he or she has a right to know that in order to take the necessary steps to wind up his or her affairs, and bring his or her life's projects to a satisfactory conclusion.[15]

In the absence of unequivocal evidence to the contrary, we ought always to presume that persons *do* want to know the truth. We do wrong in several ways by presuming that they do *not* want to know: (a) we fail to treat them as fully functioning rational persons capable of coping in their own way with reality; (b) we withhold from them the opportunity to demonstrate that they can deal with the truth, thus tending to perpetuate our paternalistic attitude and behavior toward them; and (c) we undermine their chances of being in a position to make rational decisions based on the best information available and hence to carry out their plans most effectively, thus undermining their self-determination and possibly also their future self-esteem and/or well-being.

With regard to workers' right to know, general arguments about the difficulties and dangers of understanding and interpreting medical records are supplemented by claims about the technicality of, and expertise needed for interpretation of, industrial hygiene data. These arguments are easily answered. Adequate education and training in the use of hazardous substances and procedures should result in accurate understanding of the risks, precautions and emergency procedures. And the employer can provide for the company physician or other qualified person to be available to explain and interpret for the worker the information in medical and monitoring records. This explanation and interpretation cannot, however, take the place of direct worker access to the information and the right of the worker to present all of the information to a qualified person whom he or she chooses for an independent assessment.

To the extent that medical personnel are not skilled in communicating medical information to lay people, it is their responsibility to develop that skill, since people have a right to have that information, and to have it in a form that they can understand. To the extent, if any, that workers generally lack adequate basic education to understand and make use of information concerning hazards they are subject to, and their own medical condition, again, if they have the right to have that information—and I claim they do—then they have the right to an education adequate to enable them to understand it. Logically, when presented with a valid argument that leads to an implausible or unwelcome conclusion, one has two choices: accept the conclusion, or challenge one or more of the premises. Similarly here, if a right cannot be satisfied given the existing background conditions, one has two choices: surrender the right, or challenge one or more of the background conditions.[16] I do not credit the idea that workers in general simply do not have the intelligence to comprehend and act rationally on the information.

With regard to the argument that workers will become unduly alarmed, there is no doubt that they are likely to become alarmed if they learn of the hazards of the materials they work with, the levels of exposure to which they and their co-workers have been subjected, or that they themselves have abnormal lung x-rays, reduced lung function, damaged chromosomes, high levels of toxins in their blood, or whatever. "Unduly" alarmed? The assumption here, of course, is that workers would be unable to comprehend the information if they had it; they would jump to unwarranted conclusions; their imaginations would run away with them; they would suffer needless anxiety; and they would make unreasonable demands for costly and unnecessary clean-ups, precautions, and changes in production processes. This patronizing attitude of employers toward workers is, I suggest, not only unjustified, but patently self-serving.[17]

On the one hand employers insist that workers are not really concerned about health and safety (recall the Oxy vice president's claim that the employer has to sell safety), and on the other they maintain that, if they were given accurate information they would become unduly alarmed and suffer needless anxiety. By way of contrast, surveys of rank and file worker's concerns show that they give top priority to health and safety conditions, followed by contingency protections such as workers' compensation (Berman, 1978, 119).

And a number of studies indicate that access to their own records promotes patient education and permits patients to be less anxious and more ready to follow doctors' recommendations and to be more active participants in their health care (*Federal Register*, Vol. 45, no. 102, May 23, 1980, 35237).

The real issue behind that of the right to know (and workplace health and safety generally) is control of the workplace. Employers correctly foresee that recognition and implementation of the right to know threatens to undermine what has long been recognized as the employers' prerogative to make all decisions about what to do and how to do it. It threatens also to reverse the trend of ever-increasing division and routinization of tasks with its attendant de-skilling and relative interchangeability and replaceability of workers, which in turn keeps the workforce disciplined and makes the employers' decision-making prerogative seem natural and inevitable.

Clearly, if workers are to be in a position to make rational decisions and take rational steps to protect their lives and health, they must have the relevant information. The four aspects of the right to know that we have discussed here obviously constitute part of the relevant information. But when it is recognized that relevant information includes not only the immediate dangers of substances and processes currently in use, but what alternative substances might be substituted, what different processes might be feasible, what new operations are being contemplated for the future, and so on—and that when workers have that information, they will want to have something to say about decisions based on it (as they have a right to do, since those decisions are crucial to their survival, health, and family life), then we begin to see why employers are extremely reluctant to recognize the right to know. In the long run, the issue of the right to know is inseparable from the issue of workers' control.

Thus, when employers talk about workers becoming unduly alarmed, what they really mean, I suggest, is alarmed enough to want to do something about the hazards they face, and to participate in decisions about them. The professed concern about workers suffering unnecessary anxiety, then, is paternalistic, but not in just the sense we discussed in Chapter 1. There we adopted Gerald Dworkin's characterization of paternalism as interference with the liberty of action of an individual justified by reasons referring exclusively to the good, welfare, happiness, etc., of the individual coerced.

Here we have to do with paternalism of a much broader kind. This is the kind of paternalism according to which feudalism, the slave plantation system, and the southern mill village at the turn of the century were paternalistic institutions. This kind of paternalism has at least as much to do with the control and power of the coercer as with the good, welfare, or happiness of the persons coerced. This notion of paternalism is illustrated in the following excerpt:

> In short, the mill village was an almost completely paternalistic system. Management controlled outright when, where, for how long, and for what wages the operatives worked. It exerted a substantial influence over where the operatives lived, shopped, studied, played and worshipped. In addition, management thoroughly policed the village, making sure that threats to the operatives' morality—liquor, prostitutes, and labor organizers—were kept at a safe distance. Within some villages, management even went so far as to suppress local politics so that "no mayorality elections, aldermanic squabbles," or ward politics "kept the people in ferment." State and national politics, which could not be prevented, were carefully watched. Management in such villages placed inspectors at the ballot box to see that each operative voted the right way. If an operative failed to vote for management's convictions, "he would bring down a lot of trouble upon himself." In such a tightly organized and controlled environment, any unionization attempts were necessarily predisposed to failure. [McLaurin, 1971, 38–39]

This paternalism harks back to the time when all wage earners were viewed as servants, and together with women and children (as well as slaves, idiots, and lunatics, if any), were under the protection, guidance and discipline of the paterfamilias. He was the propertied male head of household who was responsible for his dependents in all aspects of their lives. That he was responsible arose from—and enforced—the view that he was the only responsible person in the lot. He defined and represented their interests as they were presumed to be incapable of doing for themselves. We see both another illustration of this attitude and how self-serving it can be in the arguments of New England mill owners against the ten-hour day in the 1820's and 30's. One said, " Yes, I verily believe there are a large number of operatives in our cotton mills who have too much time to spare now," and shorter hours "would increase crime, suffering, wickedness and pauperism." Another announced, "It is not the hours per day that a person works that breaks him down, but the hours spent in dissipation" (Lerner, 7).

To the extent—and I think it is considerable—that remnants of this kind of paternalism influence the attitudes and behavior of employers toward workers, workers are not treated as mature, adult, responsible human beings. Not only is this demeaning to workers, it means that our purported system of individual freedom and self-determination continues to deny self-determination to the majority of people in that area of their lives that has the most profound impact on them: their work.

In most cases, withholding information from people on the grounds that they do not have the background, expertise, or sheer capacity to understand and act rationally on it is a more subtle form of this same kind of paternalism. Of course, the continued withholding of information automatically justifies the claim that those without it do not have sufficient knowledge to make decisions. This process can eventually undermine people's confidence in their own ability to make such decisions. So the whole process tends to be self-fulfilling and self-perpetuating. It is a subtle form of the kind of paternalism we have been discussing in that it attempts to justify and reinforce control of one group over another on grounds that the members of the second group are not capable of rationally and responsibly controlling themselves.

Thus the weakest claim we can make, one which seems incontestable, is that workers have the right to know, as spelled out in the four aspects with which we began this discussion: labeling, posting, personal medical records and monitoring records. This right is a necessary condition for satisfaction of the right of informed consent to exposure to workplace hazards. It is necessary for workers to make important decisions about the priorities in their lives, and for them to participate in their own health care. This information is needed for individual workers to make individual decisions about their individual and family lives.

But in addition, a stronger interpretation of the right to make decisions importantly affecting one's life leads to the claim that workers have the right to participate (and not just be consulted) in decisions concerning what is done and how it is done at work. This stronger interpretation is justified, I claim, by the facts (a) that the range of options generally available to the individual worker on an individual basis does not allow for meaningful self-determination on that basis alone, and (b) that what is done and how it is done all day (or night) at work profoundly influences all other aspects of one's life, such as health, safety, security, personality, family life, leisure activities, and self-esteem.[18] Any reasonable interpretation of the right to make (or participate meaningfully in) decisions that importantly affect one's life must, therefore, include decisions about what goes on

at work. And, of course, the information involved in the four aspects of the right to know issue is a part of the information necessary for exercising this right.

Thus, workers have the right to know because this right is a necessary condition for them to make for themselves certain decisions and to participate fully in other decisions that crucially affect their lives. The right of self-determination is, at least in large part, the right to make some and participate in most other decisions importantly affecting one's life.[19] This right provides an important basis for the rights of workers to decide whether or not to accept or remain in a job involving certain risks, to participate in decisions concerning the use of hazardous substances and the design of machinery and processes used in the workplace and to the information necessary for those decisions. At the same time, the fact that these information and decision-making rights are necessary for the protecion of the lives, health and safety of workers provides a practical, down-to-earth basis for some important aspects of the right of self-determination.

Three

The Case of the Burnside Foundry

In this chapter we explore the right to refuse an unsafe assignment. We argue that an effective right to refuse is a necessary condition for informed consent to workplace hazards. Noting that the right to refuse, as well as any other rights that workers have by virtue of being workers, is empty if one does not have a job, we go on to explore the claim that a person has a right to a job. We conclude by observing that the same considerations which support the claim that persons have a right to a job also support the claim that they have a right not just to any job, however demeaning, meaningless, routine, or boring, but to useful and challenging work.

The Burnside Foundry in South Chicago:

February 14: Six workers are sent home by the company for refusing to work on the furnace floor, where pools of water up to three [inches] deep have been collecting in tapping pits.

February 15: The six men return to work. They know that if any of the 3200 degree molten metal being poured from the furnace into a ladle were to make contact with the water on the floor, a tremendous explosion would rock the foundry. The company says that it will remove the water from the floor.

February 16: Molten steel is being poured from the furnace into the ladle. The ladle jams. Two maintenance men, Steve Mihalik and Lawrence Stiff, go to work on the jammed ladle. Neither has any protective clothing, face shield, or flame retardant equipment which the company is required to provide.

Suddenly the ladle unjams. The hot liquid metal spills over the side. In the tapping pit below, the three inches of water there is instantly turned into a mass of steam, expanding in volume more than one thousand times. Massive energy is released, spraying hot metal in all directions, and Mihalik, Stiff, and 18 other workers in the area suffer severe burns over their bodies.

The evening of February 16: Steve Mihalik dies from . . . burns over 90 percent of his body.

February 25: Lawrence Stiff dies, and shortly afterwards fellow steelworkers Albert Chisholm, Jr., and Lewis O'Daniel also die. Stiff, Chisholm, and O'Daniel are black.

Mihalik, 58, was the president of Local 1719 of the United Steelworkers (USWA) at Burnside. Stiff, 65, had worked in the foundry for more than 30 years, and was due to retire next month.

In the aftermath of the explosion at Burnside, Occupational Safety and Health Administration (OSHA) officials conducted a two-week investigation and then announced their findings. They found that the company had not taken adequate precautions to prevent the explosion of February 16th and levied a fine of $42,000 and ordered the company not to reopen for production until all violations are corrected.

David Marshall, secretary of the grievance committee of Local 1719, pointed out that the union has filed more than 50 grievances in the past year on safety related problems, and that a year ago two men were badly burned when the ladle overturned due to defective bearings. Two years ago, Marshall added, a worker was decapitated at Burnside when a moving crane whose operator could not see the man, swung it against him.

"The safety Committee has to have more power to deal with the company at the shop level," said Marshall. "We should be able to file charges, levy fines against the company when they violate the safety of the men, and set a time limit of eight hours for the company to correct unsafe working conditions, with the men being paid their regular hourly rate of pay while they wait for the company to make the necessary changes."

James Balanoff, director of District 31, USWA, labeled the deaths at Burnside "murder," and pledged that "if I do nothing else, I am going to bring these companies into the 20th century."

Balanoff said there have been nine deaths in District 31 plants in the past year, with eight of them in the South Chicago area.

Workers in the steel mills, coal mines and other industries are demanding stronger contract clauses on safety and health; especially protection for workers who refuse to work under unsafe conditions. In addition, many workers are asking why management officials who are responsible for overseeing the carrying out of safe working conditions, should not be held liable when workers suffer death or injury due to unsafe jobs. . . . [from an article by Herb Kaye, *Daily World*, March 15, 1979]

Steel

In addition to burns, explosions, and myriad other accidents, steel foundry workers may be exposed to silica dust, carbon monoxide, resins such as phenol formaldehyde, hydrocarbon, coal tar pitch, lead (for leaded steel), galvanizing chemicals, noise and heat stress (Scott, 1974, 41). Let us look briefly at the effects of a few of these hazards.

Silica dust causes silicosis, a scarring of the lungs which causes them to become progressively inelastic, making it more and more difficult to breathe, and preventing passage of oxygen to the blood. The scars may join together and form larger scars, which may occupy the entire lung. This process, called progressive massive fibrosis, is often accompanied by increased susceptibility to tuberculosis and other lung infections. The heart, due to the strain of pumping blood through inelastic lungs, becomes enlarged and fails to pump effectively (Stellman and Daum, 1973, 167-69).

According to Rachel Scott, "Three foundries in Muskegan, Michigan, employing thirty-five hundred to four thousand men have for years produced about four hundred new cases of silicosis annually. Ten percent of the entire workforce, in other words, was disabled every year" (Scott, 1974, 41).

Carbon monoxide is a colorless and odorless gas so one can be exposed with no way of knowing it. It attaches and binds itself chemically to hemoglobin, the blood component that normally carries oxygen in the blood. If body tissues do not receive a constant supply of oxygen, they stop functioning and die. The brain is most susceptible, and early symptoms of carbon monoxide poisoning are the results of brain misfunction due to lack of oxygen. Acute symptoms: headache, then throbbing headache, reddening of the skin, dizziness, dimness of vision, nausea, vomiting, and at higher concentrations, coma, suffocation, and death. Long term, low dose effects: headaches, dizziness, decreased hearing, visual disturbances, personality changes, seizures, psychosis, palpitations of the heart with abnormal rhythms, loss of appetite, nausea and vomiting (Stellman and Daum, 1973, 164-65).

Coal tar pitch causes dermatitis accompanied by pains, swelling, rash, and blisters, skin cancer, including scrotal cancer, lung irritation, and may occasionally cause pulmonary edema (Stellman and Daum, 1973, 193-94).

In the coke ovens powdered coal is converted into coke, a hard, dense fuel that is used to charge the steel furnaces. This is the dirtiest work place in a foundry. Coke oven workers risk excessive exposure to coal tars. They develop cancer of the scrotum at a rate five times that of the general population. They also develop cancers of the lung, bladder and kidneys at rates greater than the general population (Scott, 1974, 45). A study begun in 1962 and published by the U.S.

Department of Labor in 1974 examined the health records of 100,000 steelworkers at 17 plants. Among its findings were the following: Coke workers as a group are two and one-half times more likely to die of lung cancer than steelworkers who do not work in coke plants; after five years on the job in the coke plant the lung cancer rate rises to three and one-half times the normal rate; for workers on top of the coke batteries with five years on the job, the death rate is ten times higher than normal (Spencer, 1977, 224; Scott, 1974, 45–46).

Considering these facts, it is important to note that while the overall percentage of blacks in the workforce in basic steel is 22 percent, in the coke oven area it is 90 percent. Of all black coke oven workers, 18 percent were in full-time topside jobs, compared to 3.4 percent of white coke workers *(Safer Times,* July/August, 1978, 3).

Heat stress takes various forms, depending on the conditions of exposure, degree of activity, and individual body response. There are four types of acute reaction: heat stroke, heat exhaustion, heat shock, and heat fatigue.

Heat stroke involves a sharp rise in body temperature accompanied by confusion, angry behavior, delirium, and even convulsions. The skin is warm and dry and there is no sweating. It can be fatal.

In *heat exhaustion,* or heat fainting, the victim feels tired, giddy, and nauseated, and may feel chilly. There may be rapid, shallow breathing, a weak, slow pulse, and moist, clammy, cold, pale, or even bluish skin. The blood pressure is low because the blood vessels all over the body are dilated, and there is not enough blood to circulate through these enlarged vessels.

Heat shock is a form of heat exhaustion common in healthy persons working in a hot environment to which they have not become acclimatized. The body loses excessive amounts of fluid and/or salt due to inefficient sweating. There may be insufficient fluid in the body to maintain circulation to all organs. Lack of salt may result in heat cramps, weakness, nausea, headache, fatigue, and dizziness. The victim becomes irritable and suffers muscular weakness.

Heat fatigue is characterized by the lassitude, irritability, and easy fatigability that are familiar hot weather sensations. "A person with heat fatigue does not work as well, produces less, makes more mistakes, and has more accidents. The feelings get worse if the fatigue is not relieved by rest. Heat fatigue may affect a person's personal relations on the job and at home as well. Thus in addition to paying a physical price for working in a hot environment, a worker will pay an emotional price" (Stellman and Daum, 1973, 128).

Prolonged exposure to a hot environment results in a process called acclimatization. The process takes from four to six days and is most effective in young people; older people never acclimatize to heat completely. Changes occur in the circulatory system and in the volume and composition of sweat. Dilation of the small blood vessels of the skin allows the heat of the blood to be transferred through the skin back to the environment. This increases the work load for the heart since blood must be pumped through a larger total circulation area. To compensate for this increased work load, the blood vessels to the liver, stomach, and intestines constrict. The liver is sometimes damaged by lack of oxygen resulting from prolonged active work in a hot environment (Stellman and Daum, 1973, 123–28).

Discussion

Let us begin this discussion by picking up the thread of an issue that links the first three chapters and, less directly, the fourth as well. In the first chapter we raised the question whether the Cyanamid case could be called a case of sterilization without informed consent, due to lack of genuine consent. In the second chapter we raised the same question concerning the Oxy case, this time due to lack of information. We went on to explore the more general right of informed consent to risks and hazards one is exposed to on the job, and its implications for the right to know. In this chapter we shall look at the implications of the right of informed consent to risks or hazards on the job for the issue of the right of workers to refuse an unsafe work assignment.

It is not clear from the report of the Burnside Foundry case whether any of the workers who were sent home on February 14th for refusing their assignments were among those killed or injured on the 16th. It seems likely that some of them were the same, but that is not really important. What is important is whether the workers had a right to refuse to be subjected to a risk of what they believed to be a high probability of serious injury or death, and if so, what the bases of that right are, and what the right entails.

Workers have been dismissed (and told they had *quit*), fired for insubordination, suspended without pay, sent home without pay for the remainder of a shift and told not to return until ready to do the job, had disciplinary letters placed in their files (which can later be used to justify firing, not promoting, etc., on the grounds that a person is uncooperative or a troublemaker)—all for refusing assignments they believed to be unsafe. The arguments to justify these responses on the part of employers seem to be one or more of the following:

1. The employee accepted the job. This is part of the job. Therefore, the employee should do this or (a) be considered to have
   quit, or (b) be fired for insubordination for refusing to do the job
   he or she was hired to do.[1]
2. If workers are permitted to refuse assignments, plant discipline
   will break down and chaos will ensue. Therefore, workers who
   refuse must be let go or otherwise disciplined.
3. To pay workers who have refused an assignment on the grounds
   that they consider it unsafe would be to pay them for not
   working rather than for working, and surely that no employer is
   bound to do.
4. If workers had the right to be paid in such circumstances, that
   would be tantamount to a right to strike with pay, and surely
   workers do not have *that* right.

In the first argument, the assumption seems to be that in accepting
a job a person agrees to carry out any assignment falling within that
job, so to refuse an assignment is a breach of the employment
contract. There are at least two possible responses to this argument.

The first response is to deny that the unsafe assignment is part of
the job. An assignment that poses a serious threat to life, health, or
safety cannot be said to fall within the definition of any job except for
those where extreme risks are expressly understood in advance. Even
so, this is a matter of degree. Coal miners daily face risks most
workers do not face simply by entering the mines. But if a tunnel
ceiling has not been properly inspected and repaired, the fact that
they have agreed to the risk of working underground cannot be used
to argue that they breach that agreement if they refuse to enter a shaft
that does not meet legally required—or other reasonable—safety
standards.[2] A stunt person agrees to accept risks that other actors are
not expected, and would rightfully refuse, to face. But if a stunt
person regards a particular stunt as poorly designed, or believes
crucial safety equipment to be defective, he or she can rightfully say
that *those* risks are *not* part of the job. According to this response, a
crucial premise of the first argument is denied.

The second response does not deny that the assignment in question is part of the job. It points out that the employer has the legal and
moral and often contractual obligation to provide a safe and healthy
work environment. So it is the employer, not the employee, who has
breached the employment agreement or contract.[3] Still, many collective bargaining agreements contain grievance procedures, and a
worker who alleges that the employer is in violation of the contract is
normally expected to file a grievance and proceed with his or her

assigned work.[4] This approach is obviously inadequate in the case of a serious and immediate threat to life, health, or safety. Thus it is the seriousness and immediacy of the threat that supports the right to refuse. Such refusal is not itself a breach of the employment agreement, however; rather it is a response—the only adequate response available—to a breach by the employer.

Either way, there is no justification for claiming that, by refusing an unsafe assignment an employee either breaches the employment agreement or is insubordinate.[5] It cannot be that, in accepting a job, one consents to all risks and hazards that may be encountered in that job. To be meaningful, the right of informed consent must apply at two levels. Before accepting a job and while remaining in it, one has the right to the information needed for informed consent to the risks that the job entails. One must also have the right to refuse a particular assignment one believes to constitute a serious and immediate threat to one's life, health or safety. And note that the right to know is an indispensable part of the right of informed consent at both levels. Both the right of informed consent and the right to a safe job are, in practical terms, empty if the price of refusing an unsafe assignment may be one's job. Indeed, these rights, along with all other rights of workers are relatively empty in the absence of an effective right to a job. This is so in several ways, as we shall see below.

We have, I believe, disposed of the first of the employer arguments against the right to refuse. But what of the second argument, that if workers are permitted to refuse assignments, plant discipline will break down and chaos will result? We might look at the experience elsewhere, for example in Canada, where legislation passed in seven provinces during the 1970's guarantees the right to refuse:

> Fears by management that health and safety issues would be exaggerated out of proportion or used to further other collective bargaining goals have not been borne out. In 1500 cases of work refusal in Saskatchewan, all cases were considered to be legitimate by Saskatchewan authorities. Experience has also shown that the increased worker participation in making actual operational decisions on health and safety has reduced potential for industrial conflict, in addition to raising awareness about safety. [*NJCOSH Newsletter*, May 1979, 1]

In Saskatchewan, the right to refuse is held by individual workers, though groups of individual workers can exercise it together. The worker or any member of the legally mandated union-management health and safety committee can call in an inspector to arbitrate if there is a dispute. (According to provincial officials, that occurs in fewer than five percent of the cases.) The inspector is required to render a decision as soon as possible, usually within twenty-four hours. If an employer feels that the worker did not have "reasonable grounds" to believe the situation was "unusually dangerous," the employer must prove it before disciplinary action can be taken. The employee must receive normal pay and benefits until the issue is settled. Even so, Jennie Smyth of the provincial safety division reports, "The right to refuse has been underused rather than over-used. There have been many situations we hear of later in which people should have refused but were afraid to" (Witt and Early, 1980, 25).

Workers in Sweden also have a strong right to refuse. Individual workers have the right to refuse dangerous work, and the government mandated safety committee (more than half of whose members must be elected by nonsupervisory employees) can shut down unsafe operations.[6] They can be overruled only by a government inspector. Even if overruled, no worker can be punished for exercising the right to refuse unsafe work or stop an unsafe operation unless the action was taken in bad faith. Swedish central labor confederation attorneys report that they know of not a single case in which a worker has been prosecuted for deliberate abuse of these rights. Since the right of safety committees to stop dangerous work went into effect in 1974, use of it has resulted in the intervention of government inspectors only about twenty-five times per year in the country's 160,000 work-places (Witt and Early, 1980, 25).

Considering that the right to refuse is vital to the effectiveness of the right to a safe job and to the right of informed consent to job hazards, the case against the right to refuse would have to be very strong indeed to justify its denial. That some unjustified refusals might occur would certainly not be sufficient reason. Yet there seems to be no reason to assume that workers would abuse the right to refuse, and experience where the right has been in effect for some years argues against the assumption. Thus the second employer argument fails.

The third argument is not directed against the right to refuse itself, but against the obligation of employers to pay workers who have refused an assignment on the grounds that it is unsafe. One potential buttress for this argument, that paying workers who have refused would lead to massive abuse of the right to refuse, is not plausible in light of the Canadian and Swedish experiences. Thus the argument must rest on the claim that it would be an injustice to the employer to require that a worker be paid after refusing an assignment, for this would require the employer to pay the worker for not working.

Many union contracts in the United States actually provide for the right of a worker to refuse an unsafe assignment, but do not guarantee that the worker will not sacrifice his or her earnings by doing so. The result is that the right is seldom invoked. In the course of discussing one case in which it was successfully invoked at a Republic steel plant, Charles Spencer writes:

Article Twelve reads: "If an employee shall believe there exists an unsafe condition . . . so that the Employee is in danger of injury . . . the Employee shall have the right . . . to be relieved from duty on the job in respect to which he has complained and to return to such job when the unsafe condition shall be remedied."

It's not as simple as it reads. It's a bewildering and uncoordinated procedure that can be disastrous to any worker who invokes it. In the thirty years it has been a part of the union contract, it has never [until this occasion] been successful in correcting a single unsafe working condition—which accounts for the shift towards dependence on federal government intervention. Almost identical provisions are written into all union contracts,[7] and the experience has been much the same.

Requesting to be relieved from duty until an unsafe condition shall be remedied runs into such hurdles as (1) is there *really* an unsafe condition? who says so? (2) what's to happen to the workers "relieved from duty" if there's no other work available? They can't be paid for staying home. (3) who shall decide if the unsafe condition has actually been remedied? (4) what happens to the other workers who aren't complaining and are willing to continue on the job?

There had been numerous instances at this plant where workers who invoked Article Twelve and requested to be relieved from duty on the job until an unsafe condition is remedied were "furloughed" for several weeks, during which they were not paid a penny and in the meantime other workers were assigned to and performed the same job. If the newly assigned workers had refused, they, too, could have been disciplined, even discharged. Although Article Twelve provides for the Company to reassign workers to another job when they invoke Article Twelve, it is the usual contention of the Company that no other job is available. [Spencer, 1977, 213–14]

Another more subtle way in which workers are discouraged from exercising the right to refuse is explained in Rachel Scott's report of an interview with Ken Bellett, a steelworker at Bethlehem's Lackawanna plant:

The men themselves sometimes "forsake safety," he said, to make production. "Most workers are on some kind of incentive program. Every department has a different kind of incentive. Foremen are also on incentive and top management have a bonus system. Under contract terms, a man can refuse to do the job because it's unsafe. The guy will holler but then go ahead and do it. Otherwise, he's going to lose money that day. It's going to affect his earnings. If it means shutting down a whole department, the other guys will shoot you." The result is that often rather than shutting machinery down for repairs, maintenance workers have to work while it is operating. [Scott, 1974, 57–58]

Recall that two days prior to the fatal explosion at the Burnside foundry six workers were sent home for refusing to work near the pools of water in the tapping pits. Six workers lost their pay for the remainder of a shift, the unsafe condition was not corrected, and four workers lost their lives. Workers generally cannot afford to continue to refuse until a job is made safe. In part this is because, as long as it is the worker who is bearing the cost, if the employer can keep the operation going without the worker in question, the employer need be in no hurry at all to correct the unsafe situation. And a worker whose refusal would result in the shutting down of an operation faces not only his or her loss of earnings, but that of his or her co-workers as well. So the employer can rest assured that this will rarely happen.

In view of these considerations, it seems clear that the right to refuse an unsafe assignment cannot be effective unless (a) the worker's normal pay is continued after the refusal, (b) some person or group representing the workers, such as a safety steward or safety committee has the power to shut down an unsafe operation with no loss of pay to the affected workers, and (c) incentive programs such as those described by Bellett are eliminated or somehow revised so that workers are not constantly forced to make a trade-off between safety and earnings. Condition (c) appears to be necessary both directly, and as a necessary condition for (a) and (b).

A worker can, of course, complain to OSHA to get an unsafe situation corrected, but there are several reasons why this is no substitute for a strong and effective right to refuse. First, although OSHA attempts to inspect within twenty-four hours situations in which the area director determines that there is a reasonable basis for the claim of "imminent danger," there is always some delay. The potential length of delay has been greatly increased by the Supreme Court's 1978 *Barlow* decision ruling that an employer may require an OSHA inspector to obtain a search warrant before entering the premises. If the worker stands to lose pay during that time, he or she is still in the position of choosing between economic loss which the worker may not be able to afford and doing the unsafe job for some period of time until an inspector arrives. If the inspector finds an imminent danger, he or she asks the employer voluntarily to abate the hazard and remove endangered employees from the area. If the employer refuses, OSHA, through the regional solicitor, applies to the nearest Federal District Court for appropriate legal action. Thus the potential for substantial delay is clearly present.

In addition, OSHA gives top priority only to inspecting situations where the area director determines that there is reasonable basis for the claim of "imminent danger." An "imminent danger" is defined in Section 13(a) of the OSH Act as "any condition where there is reasonable certainty that a danger exists that can be expected to cause death or serious physical harm immediately or before the danger can be eliminated through normal enforcement procedures" (Nothstein, 1981, 295–96). A "serious violation," which is not top, but third priority for inspection, exists under Section 17(k) "if there is a substantial probability that death or serious physical harm could result . . . " (Nothstein, 1981, 347). There are obvious difficulties in distinguishing in practice between an imminent danger and a serious violation, so defined. A boiler about to explode is an imminent danger, but a boiler dangerously in need of repair could explode now or could rumble along for another six months or more. That it was about to explode is, I would guess, in the vast majority of cases, known only after the fact. Moreover, there are other problems about what constitutes an imminent danger. Health hazards, for example, are imminent dangers under the Act if there is a reasonable expectation that toxic substances or dangerous fumes, dusts, or gases are present and that exposure to them will cause irreversible harm to such a degree as to shorten life or cause reduction in physical or mental efficiency, even though the resulting harm is not immediately apparent (Nothstein, 1981, 296). Yet when the Oil, Chemical and Atomic Workers International Union claimed that pools of mercury on the floor of an Allied Chemical factory represented an imminent danger, and showed that at least twenty-five workers in the area had symptoms (tingling in hands and feet, tremors, irritability, drowsiness, loss of memory, and sore gums) or chemical evidence of mercury poisoning, the Department of Labor ruled that "imminent danger" applied only when there was a "risk of sudden great physical harm . . . like a boiler explosion" (Stellman and Daum, 1973, 12).[8]

For these reasons, and because it seems to me that "substantial probability that death or serious physical harm could result," can be sufficient to warrant refusal, I believe that a worker's right to refuse cannot be limited to imminent danger situations. It must apply also to serious violations and to serious hazards that are not violations of specific OSHA (or other relevant) standards. But in the case of a serious violation, not only will there be a longer delay before an inspection, the employer will normally be given some period of time (possibly days, possibly months) in which to correct the violation while continuing in operation. An employer can then appeal any aspect of the citation, arguing, for example, that the situation is not a violation at all, or that it cannot be corrected in the time alloted. This can drag the process out still further. Or an employer can simply fail to correct the violation, the fine that may result usually being much less than the cost of correction.

Now one response to all this is that OSHA's enforcement system should be strengthened. There should be more compliance officers, and they should have, and use, greater enforcement powers, especially in the case of imminent dangers and serious violations. This is certainly true.[9] But such enforcement should be a complement to an effective right to refuse.

It is worth noting in this connection that there had been an OSHA inspection several months before the fatal explosion at the Burnside foundry. Workers had pointed out to the inspector the pools of water in the tapping pit. The water was not cited as a violation in the inspection report (*CACOSH Health & Safety News*, Vol. 6, no. 8, 1). Yet, after the explosion, OSHA officials conducted a two-week investigation and among the violations cited were these:

—Workers were required to work with and transfer molten steel and slag from furnaces to ladles where the material could contact water and wet surfaces.

—Water was allowed to seep into the tapping pits by improper maintenance of ground water draining systems and ineffective sealing of pit sides and bottom.

—During the weeks preceeding February 16th, the furnace tapping pits were not cleaned, thus allowing water pockets to occur and increase the amount of water which would not be pumped out.

—The company did not provide adequate personal protective equipment to prevent exposure of maintenance workers to the hazards of burns.

—Repairs to a defective ladle tilting mechanism were attempted while the ladle was suspended over the tapping pit. [Kaye, 1979, 22]

The company was ordered not to reopen until all the violations were corrected.

One point this illustrates is that in many ways the workers themselves are the real experts concerning health and safety problems and hazards in their workplaces. They are there all day, day after day, year after year. They see, hear about, and experience directly the accidents, near misses, headaches, sore throats, difficulty breathing, and the rest. Providing workers with whatever technical training is necessary, and empowering them to enforce their right to a safe and healthy workplace by means of an effective right to refuse an unsafe assignment, and to shut down an unsafe operation, is thus an eminently sensible approach to workplace health and safety. It cannot work, however, if it is not backed up by government intervention and enforcement in disputed cases. A strengthened OSHA enforcement system is needed as a complement. This would be a primarily *preventive* approach in two senses. It would be more likely to prevent injuries, deaths and illnesses than a system which can only respond more slowly and often after the fact. In addition, the more effective the power to shut down an unsafe operation, the less likely workers would be to have to use it in order to get hazards corrected.

To illustrate, let us look again at the Swedish experience:

> The degree of incentive for managers to reach agreement with workers on health and safety issues depends, of course, on the remedies available to workers. . . .
>
> Since the right of safety committees to stop dangerous work was established in Sweden in 1974, use of it has required the intervention of government inspectors only about twenty-five times per year in the country's 160,000 workplaces. All parties interviewed agreed that this low figure was mainly a reflection of the effectiveness of the threat of using that power, and not a reflection of workers' reluctance to use it or of ignorance of their rights.
>
> According to Bo Feldt, chief union safety committee member at the 12,000-worker Volvo plant at Göteborg:
>
>> We have over 200 safety stewards in the plant and their strength is in their ability to go to the foremen and say, "Do that or I stop the job." The foremen usually do it—whatever it is. If the men stop work, even if the government comes in and says work should continue, they can't be punished. But our experience has been that most of the stops have been correct stops. [Witt and Early, 1980, 25]

As we have seen, all of the incentives presently at work in our system seem to weigh against the employee exercising the right to refuse, and against the employer responding by correcting the condition promptly when the right is exercised. The requirement that employees be paid in the event of a refusal or a shutdown of unsafe work should help to shift that balance, removing a strong disincentive to workers' exercising the right to refuse, and providing an incentive for the employer to act promptly to correct the condition so as to prevent or end a shutdown.

But, it may be objected, if there really is no other available work to assign the workers, would it not be unjust to require the employer to pay them? If it is unjust, then even if it would probably have desirable consequences, it may not be justifiable. The objection has not been satisfied.

My response is that it is not unjust. A worker is hired to do a job and shows up prepared to do it. He or she has a right to a safe environment in which to do the job. If that is not provided, the employer has failed to fulfill the employment agreement, as I argued in response to the first employer argument. What would be unjust would be for the worker, who has fulfilled his or her side of the agreement, to be forced to bear the financial loss resulting from the employer's failure to do the same.

Now it will be objected that I am assuming that the worker's claim that the assignment is unsafe is true, but often that is just what is at issue.

It seems to me that the worker must be given the benefit of the doubt in this situation. For one thing, it is his or her life that is at stake if the condition really is unsafe. The right of self-determination requires that a decision so importantly affecting his or her life be made by the individual. Moreover, the right to refuse could not be effective if the worker stood the chance of losing pay, or even his or her job, because the situation is later found not to have been unsafe. The worker might, of course, be right and still be "found" wrong. Or the worker may be wrong but have had good reason to believe the situation unsafe. So long as a worker believes in good faith that doing the work assigned would seriously threaten his or her life, health, or safety, the worker has, I claim, the right to refuse until the assignment is shown to be safe.

There may, of course, be occasions where a worker sincerely believes an assignment to be unsafe but does not have what other informed persons would regard as good reasons for that belief. I want to claim that the right to refuse without punishment or loss of earnings applies in such a case through an inspection and appeal process such as that outlined below. The distinction between good faith belief and good reason for the belief is implicitly recognized by not claiming for every individual worker the right to shut down an operation he or she believes to be unsafe. The individual worker has the right to refuse for him or herself, and to have a trained safety steward or committee with the power to shut the operation down. Obviously, there may be difficulties in determining that an individual's belief is sincere in the absence of what informed and reasonable others regard as good reason for the belief. Nevertheless, I am sure that there could be cases in which the belief was obviously sincere, though ill founded. Partly because of this indeterminacy, the burden should be on the employer to show that a refusal or stoppage was not in good faith.

None of this would be an undue burden on the employer if the issues could be resolved quickly. The Canadian and Swedish laws provide a model for how this can be accomplished. We need (a) prompt inspection and resolution of any disputed refusal or shutdown situation (within twenty-four hours, say); (b) an accelerated appeals process available to both employer and workers (another twenty-four hours); (c) workers' pay and benefits continue as usual; (d) workers not subject to penalty for being wrong, but only for acting in bad faith; and (e) any penalty to be imposed only after the employer has demonstrated to the satisfaction of the appropriate reviewing body that the refusal or shutdown was not in good faith.

That such a system is not unworkable seems amply demonstrated by the fact that some like it are in operation elsewhere. That it would require the commitment of additional resources to health and safety administration is probably true. But again, the experiences in Canada and Sweden do not suggest that such a system would result in an unmanageable flood of refusals. Some such system seems a necessary condition for an effective right to refuse an unsafe assignment, which in turn is a necessary condition for satisfaction of the right to a safe job and the right of informed consent to job hazards.

What of the employer argument that the right to be paid after refusing an assignment would be tantamount to a right to strike with pay?

The right to strike is the right to engage, with one's co-workers, in the concerted action of withholding one's labor in an attempt to achieve some common goal. The withholding of labor here is an economic tool or weapon used in an attempt to wring some concession from the employer, or force the employer to honor some right of the employees on pain of loss of income resulting from halted operations. This right is guaranteed by Section 7 of the National Labor Relations Act of 1935, commonly called the Wagner Act.

Section 502 of the Wagner Act states: "Nor shall the quitting of labor by an employee or employees in good faith because of abnormally dangerous conditions for work at the place of employment of such employee or employees be deemed a strike." This distinction seems to me well-founded. In the case of refusing an unsafe assignment or shutting down an unsafe operation, workers are not using their refusal in an attempt to get the employer to honor their right to a safe job (though one may hope that it will have this effect). They are simply *exercising* their right to a safe job, which they cannot do, under the circumstances, without withholding their labor. The right to a safe and healthful workplace includes the right not to be exposed to unreasonable risks to life or health. So, in the same way that one exercises one's right not to incriminate oneself by refusing to answer questions one would otherwise be obliged to answer, one can exercise one's right to a safe and healthful workplace by refusing work assignments that involve unreasonable risks to life or health—assignments one would otherwise be obliged, under the employment contract, to accept. The withholding of labor is not used as an instrument or weapon at all in such a case. The purpose of such a refusal is not to bring economic pressure to bear on the employer; it is simply to avoid exposure to unreasonable risk.

Thus we must distinguish between refusing an unsafe assignment and shutting down an unsafe operation on the one hand, and striking (including striking over health and safety issues) on the other. A strike over health and safety issues might occur in an effort to get strong health and safety provisions in a contract, or to enforce existing legal or contractual health or safety provisions that are being violated, where the violation does not present a serious and immediate threat to life, safety or health. Workers might strike to obtain access to information needed for a research or educational project on health and safety. Finally, workers may have shut down an operation they deemed unsafe, and gone through a process such as that outlined above, with inspection, ruling, appeal and final ruling. This much, I claim, they have the right to do without loss of pay, and this much does not constitute a strike. If, now, they are dissatisfied with the final ruling and want to try to get the employer to make the repairs or changes they deem necessary for a safe operation, they may strike in an effort to achieve this.

I have argued that workers have a moral right to refuse an unsafe assignment and to have an individual or committee representing workers empowered to shut down an unsafe operation, and they have a right to these things without loss of pay. I have attempted to counter employer arguments against the right to refuse and against the right to be paid after refusing. I shall now report, briefly and without comment, the current legal status in the United States of the right to refuse.

In 1973, The Department of Labor issued Interpretive Rule 1977.12(b) (2) which states that under the OSH Act an employee may refuse an assignment if the employee's apprehension is of such nature that a reasonable person, under the circumstances then confronting the employee, would have concluded that there is a real danger of death or serious injury and there is insufficient time, due to the urgency of the situation, to eliminate the danger through resort to regular statutory enforcement channels.

The regulation prohibits employer discrimination against workers who exercise this right.

Employers continued to take action against workers who refused assignments on safety grounds, and challenged the regulation in resulting court cases. They argued that when Congress passed the OSH Act it rejected a provision which would have authorized workers to refuse unsafe assignments without loss of pay, and that the regulation would grant workers the right to strike with pay. They warned that the right to refuse would foster disharmony in the workplace, invite continuous labor unrest, and even industrial combat. Lower courts had ruled in conflicting ways on various cases involving the right to refuse, so the legal status of the right was in limbo until February 26, 1980.

On that day the Supreme Court ruled on a case stemming from a July 10, 1974 refusal of two maintenance workers employed by Whirlpool to climb onto a guard screen suspended twenty feet above the work area. Several workers had been injured in falls through the screen, and two weeks before the refusal another worker had fallen to his death. OSHA had ordered the screen repaired, but no repairs had been made. When the men refused, they were sent home for the remaining six hours of their shift and letters of reprimand were placed in their files.

The Supreme Court unanimously upheld the interpretive regulation, saying that it "clearly conforms to the fundamental objective of the Act—to prevent occupational death and serious injuries." "It would seem anomalous," wrote Associate Justice Potter Stewart, "to construe an act so directed and constructed as prohibiting an employee, with no other reasonable alternative, the freedom to withdraw from a workplace environment that he reasonably believes is highly dangerous." The letters of reprimand were ordered withdrawn as they violated the prohibition against discriminatory action. The Court declined to rule on the issue of the six hours' pay the two men lost, saying that issue was "not before the court." The pay issue was sent back to district court to be reheard in the light of the Supreme Court's ruling.[10]

There is, as far as I know, no legal provision for workers, whether individual workers, safety stewards or committees, to shut down an unsafe operation, though some union contracts may contain such provisions. The original version of the "imminent danger" clause of the OSH Act allowed compliance officers to close down an operation in which an imminent danger was found. But the final version requires that, if the employer will not shut down voluntarily, OSHA must go to federal court.

Let me close this part of the discussion by trying to pull together what we now can say about the notion of informed consent. It probably is not possible to specify *sufficient* conditions for informed consent either in general or in relation to specific sorts of risks or activities such as workplace hazards, participation in scientific experiments, undergoing surgery, and so on. There are too many different kinds of factors which could be present in individual circumstances and which could undermine the adequacy of information or the genuineness of consent. One could not hope to think of all such possible factors and deal with them in advance. But, if what has been said on the subject in this and the preceding chapters is correct, we can say what several *necessary* conditions are for informed consent to job-related hazards or risks:

1. The offer to the potential or actual employee that he or she may accept or keep the job must not be a coercive offer. (There may be different accounts of what constitutes a coercive offer, as we noted in Chapter One, but that the offer must not be coercive for consent to be genuine should not be controversial.)
2. The employee must not be unnecessarily unfree to a high degree, as that notion is sketched out in Chapter One, with respect to the choice of whether or not to accept or keep the job. (This claim is more likely to be controversial.)
3. The right to know must be satisfied in at least all four of the aspects discussed in Chapter Two. (Another aspect of the right to know will be proposed below.)
4. The right to refuse an assignment believed by the worker to present a serious and immediate threat to life or health must be effective. This requires that the workers not be subject to discipline, loss of job or earnings, and that a person or group in the workplace, representing workers, be empowered to shut down an unsafe operation without loss of pay to the affected workers.

Two additional candidates for inclusion are the right to advance notice of, and the right to veto or require changes in proposed new machinery, materials and work procedures for health and safety reasons. These rights are held by the Swedish joint safety committees mentioned above, which must have a majority of their members elected by the non-supervisory employees. These rights are clearly related to informed consent, but it might be argued that they go somewhat beyond the notion of informed consent into the more general area of self-determination, that is, participation in decisions which importantly affect one's life. In defense of the claim that they do come under informed consent, it might be pointed out that, without these rights, new machinery, materials, and processes often are introduced into the workplace with little or no prior notice, so that workers have no opportunity to explore, in advance of using them, what the risks and hazards might be. Hence, they cannot be said to have been accorded the right of informed consent with respect to these new factors introduced into the work environment. Moreover, once the new equipment or process is in place it may be impossible— it will certainly be more difficult and expensive—to make appropriate changes or choose a safer alternative. I would, therefore, claim that the right to advance notice is clearly a necessary condition of informed consent. The right to veto or require changes in plans might go beyond informed consent, but only on the assumption, or to the degree, that conditions (1) and (2) on the above list are satisfied. Indeed, I would add that the worker must not be unfree to a high degree, *whether or not* that lack of freedom was necessary.

Remaining in a job after a new hazard has been introduced can be said to constitute consent to that hazard only if a worker is free to quit. The fewer alternatives available to a worker, for whatever reasons, the less free that worker is to quit. The less free the worker is to quit, the more is the right to veto or require modifications in proposed new processes or materials a necessary condition for consent.

I said above that the right of informed consent and the right to a safe job, along with all other rights of workers, are relatively empty in the absence of an effective right to a job. Let us now explore some of the ways in which this is so.

First, the rights to informed consent and to a safe job have no application in the case of a worker who cannot get a job at all.

Second, the right to a safe job, or any other right, is empty in the absence of effective guarantees against reprisals resulting from the exercise or attempted enforcement of the right. Employers are prohibited from discriminating against employees for exercising the rights guaranteed them under the Occupational Safety and Health Act and under the National Labor Relations Act. But workers know that employers can and often do cite other reasons for a dismissal or other disciplinary action, and there is no way to be sure one will get a favorable ruling if one contests the action. Most important, the employer's position prevails unless and until it is overturned by the relevant authority. And such a process will take months at a minimum, more likely years. The employer has every incentive for dragging the case out in the hopes that the worker will become discouraged and drop it. Meanwhile, the worker is without any means of support, and all benefits such as health insurance are cut off. The prospect of back pay in the event of a favorable ruling, especially since one cannot count on it, is no help in paying rent and buying food. Thus the threat of dismissal is an extremely powerful deterrent to a worker's exercising *any* rights against the employer's wishes, despite legal "safeguards." Reversing the burden of proof, so to speak, in dismissal and other discipline cases could go a long way toward alleviating this problem (and would, in effect, acknowledge that workers have a right to due process in disciplinary matters generally, and property rights in their jobs which may not be set aside without due process).[11]

In general, a strong union is much more effective at ensuring that workers may exercise their legal, as well as their contractual, rights than the courts or government agencies. The latter are useful, even essential, to a union's efforts in many cases, but they often are not very useful to the individual without union representation. This is so in part because of the problems of burden of proof and delay mentioned above, in part because, if the individual still has his or her job, filing a complaint is likely to bring further reprisals, including possible dismissal, in part because the individual is unlikely to have access to the kind of experienced legal advice and assistance needed to see the effort through successfully, and finally because the personal, emotional, as well as financial, cost of pursuing such a matter on one's own can be unendurable. Thus, effective rights relating to unionization are frequently necessary conditions in practice for the enforcement and exercise of even those rights provided by law for all workers whether or not they are union members. It is no wonder, therefore, that rights relating to unionization are among those rights the exercise of which is most likely to result in reprisals, as we shall see in the next chapter.

A third way in which the right to a job can be a necessary condition for the enforcement and exercise of other rights is that, in addition to individual workers facing the threat of dismissal or other disciplinary action, an entire work-force may face the threat of a shutdown or runaway shop. Getting OSHA, or other agencies at local, state, or federal levels, to set and enforce strong standards for the protection of the health and safety, or other rights, of workers is no victory for those workers whose employers' response is to pick up and move to a city, state, or country with weaker regulations, or none at all. Just like the individual worker who faces the threat of dismissal for refusing an unsafe assignment, workers who face the implicit or explicit threat of a shutdown or run-away shop in response to health and safety demands confront the choice: risk your life and health on your job.[12] This is not an idle threat. Between 1969 and 1976, fifteen million jobs were lost as a result of plant shutdowns (DeCarvalho *et al.*, 1981, 1). And, of course, the difficulties of an individual worker who loses his or her job are multiplied by much more than just the number of workers affected by a whole plant closing. The prospects of finding another job in the area are far worse. An entire community can be devastated by the closing of a major plant.

I do not deny, by the way, that small and economically marginal businesses may sometimes be forced to close by even relatively small increases in costs. The Small Business Administration does make low interest loans to help small businesses finance costs of compliance with health and safety regulations. More should be done along these lines. It should not fall on the workers to sacrifice their health and safety to save their jobs. These small and marginal businesses are not the main problem in the current wave of shutdowns and run-aways, however. According to MIT economist Bennett Harrison, "Globe-trotting corporations will close profit-making plants if they aren't profitable enough, and if they can make more elsewhere." He notes that Sperry Rand closed a plant in Herkimer, New York, because it wasn't making a 22 percent return-on-investment. Large conglomerates make money by buying out an independent company, "milking" the profits out of it, and then shutting it down. Then they get federal and state tax breaks for investing in new equipment and relocating. A study of the New England economy by Harrison and a colleague revealed that 100,000 businesses closed in New England between 1969 and 1976, costing a million jobs. Big corporations account directly for 15 percent of the shutdowns and over half of the job losses. But, in addition, many of the small independent businesses that close down do so in the wake of corporate shutdowns rippling through their communities (Dreier, 1980, 18).

Even a strong and militant union is largely defenseless against this threat, given the current legal situation in the United States. Our laws generally protect a company's right unilaterally to make all "investment" decisions. Yet this right is increasingly being questioned in view of the effects of such decisions on the lives of so many others.

When the United Steelworkers of America filed suit to block a plant closing in Youngstown, Ohio, the court said:

> This Court has spent many hours searching for a way to cut to the heart of the economic reality—that obsolescence and market forces demand the close of the Mahoning Valley plants, and yet the lives of 3500 workers and their families and the supporting Youngstown community cannot be dismissed as inconsequential. United States Steel should not be permitted to leave the Youngstown area devastated after drawing from the lifeblood of the community for so many years.
>
> Unfortunately, the mechanism to reach this ideal settlement, to recognize this new property right, is not now in existence in the code of laws of our nation. At this moment, proposals for legislative redress of economic relocation like the situation before us are pending on Capitol Hill. Perhaps labor unions, now more aware of the importance of this problem, will begin to bargain for relocation adjustment funds and mechanisms and will make such measures part of the written labor contract. However, this Court is not a legislative body and cannot make laws where none exist—only those remedies prescribed in the statutes or by virtue of precedent of prior case law can be given cognizance. In these terms this Court can determine no legal basis for the finding of a property right.[13]

The court here clearly recognizes the existence of a moral right of workers to their jobs. The right referred to here is a kind of property right, acquired, presumably, by working at a particular job. Legal recognition and protection of this right is a necessary condition for the protection of other worker rights. As the existence of this right becomes more widely recognized, there will no doubt be much controversy over precisely what it amounts to. I shall not attempt to resolve that question here. It may be useful, however, in thinking about the question, to see how some other countries are handling it, and what some proposed legislation in the United States looks like.

Sweden, West Germany, and the United Kingdom all have national legislation regulating plant closings and reductions in force (layoffs). Typically, corporations are legally required to give advance notice to the national employment service, the union or works council, and the individual employees likely to be affected before closing a plant or dismissing workers for economic reasons. The amount of notice varies among the countries, and depending on the number of workers affected and the body being notified. Before implementing such a decision (and in some cases, before finalizing it), the company must negotiate with the employees' union or the plant's works council concerning possible alternative plans as well as the timing, distribution, and compensation above the statutory minimum for any layoffs that do take place. If no agreement can be reached, the matter goes to arbitration. Workers are entitled to time off with pay to look for new jobs, and for retraining in addition to severance pay, the minimum amount of which is established by statute and is pegged to the amount of time the worker has been employed by the company. In some cases the combination of notice and negotiation results in an alternative to the proposed closing or cutback being found. Often, the process is stretched out sufficiently so that a planned reduction is handled by attrition and no dismissals are necessary. When workers do lose their jobs, the proportion of income replacement provided by statutory unemployment benefits in the three countries is far higher than in the United States, payments to their Social Security accounts are continued on their behalf, and medical coverage, provided by the national health care system, continues. Interestingly, the United States is the only industrialized country besides South Africa without national health insurance.[14]

The National Employment Priorities Act was introduced in the United States Congress in 1979. If enacted, it would require advance notification by companies planning to close or relocate plants. The amount of notice varies from six months to two years, depending on the number of employees to be affected. A National Employment Priorities Administration would be created within the Department of Labor. The Administration would investigate any proposed closing or transfer and recommend ways to avoid the closing or to minimize its impact on employees and the community. It would not have the power to prevent the closing or to conciliate disputed issues between employers and employees. Employees would have the right to transfer to another facility of the same company at the same rate of pay. All relocation and retraining costs would be paid by the company or the federal government. If transfers were not available, the employer would be required to pay affected workers severance pay amounting to 85 percent of their average wage minus unemployment compensation for up to 52 weeks. Retraining programs would be provided for affected workers. Workers over the age of fifty would have the right to retire on reduced benefits. Pension and health insurance payments for all affected workers would be guaranteed for one year. The affected community would receive a mandatory one-time payment of 85 percent of the resulting annual tax loss.

Less comprehensive bills have been introduced in several state legislatures, including those of Ohio, Massachusetts, Pennsylvania, and Illinois. Clearly, federal legislation would be preferable, as states and municipalities often end up competing with each other, to the detriment of all of them, by offering concessions to businesses, such as tax abatement schemes, lax environmental standards, anti-union "right to work" laws, and a generally "favorable climate for business," in order to attract companies (and hence jobs) or persuade them not to leave.[15] The textile industry, for example, has virtually deserted New England, relocating either in the "Sunbelt," where few workers are unionized and wages are the lowest in the country, or in "developing" countries such as South Korea, Taiwan, and the Philipines. In these countries, repressive regimes friendly to U.S. business guarantee low wages, a well-disciplined workforce, and few or no health and safety or environmental regulations. Indeed, the lure of these countries, where daily wages correspond to hourly wages in the United States, is so great that even the "Sunbelt" is losing some eighty jobs due to plant closings for every one hundred jobs created there (*Economic Notes*, Vol. 48, No. 5). Thus it is necessary that workers' rights be nationally, and indeed internationally, guaranteed and protected if workers are not to be faced constantly with the threat that enforcing and exercising their rights as workers may cost them their very jobs.

Another approach to the protection of workers' rights to their jobs in the face of plant closings is to guarantee them and/or their community the right to buy out or take over the closed plant and run it themselves. This often would not be feasible, however, even if corporate cooperation and access to initial capital were available. One reason for this is that, as we saw above, corporations, especially conglomerates, often run a plant into the ground, failing to reinvest profits in necessary maintenance and modernization, siphoning them off into more profitable investments instead. So the doctrine that the owners of a business concern have the sole right to make decisions concerning the investment of profits from that business permits a company to let a plant deteriorate, while extracting profits from its operation, and then to abandon the plant—along with the employees and the community that have sustained the business—when it is no longer profitable. Clearly, if the right of workers to their jobs is to be protected, some restrictions on such investment decisions are needed.

Where feasible, however, this approach could be an important complement to legislation such as the National Employment Priorities Act. There are several possible variations of this approach, which could be applied individually or in various combinations.[16] One variation would involve additional legislation requiring a corporation that has decided to close a plant to sell the plant to the workers or worker-community coalition if they choose to buy it, and providing for feasibility studies and grants or no-interest loans in cases where a feasible plan exists. Another variation would be nationalization. While this has been fairly common in other countries, in the United States government financial support, while increasingly accepted, has generally allowed for the continuation of prior corporate management. Under this proposal, the workers or worker-community coalition would manage the plant.

A third variation would be an expanded use of the eminent domain doctrine, whereby a city could condemn a property and take it over for the public good, including specifically to insure job opportunities. According to the doctrine of eminent domain, the former owners must be compensated, but the proper value may be determined by a jury of community residents.

A fourth variation is where workers facing a shutdown seize a plant and continue operating it on their own—either permanently or until some other way is found to keep it open. This variation might well be a necessary step, in practice, toward getting any legal recognition of workers' right to their jobs. Historically, workers have had to exercise their rights independently of, and frequently in defiance of the law in order to gain legal recognition and protection of those rights. As we shall see in the next chapter, this was true of both the right to organize and the right to strike—and many government employees must still defy the law to exercise their right to strike.

These approaches to protection of a property right of workers in their jobs, though only partial, would be an important step toward establishing recognition of such a right, and recognition of a corresponding limitation on the right of a corporation to make investment decisions without regard for their impact on the lives of workers, their families and communities.

But there are several reasons why I want to say that the right to a job is more than a property right. Or, to put it another way, in addition to the property right of a particular worker in a particular job, there is a more general right of a person to a job. One reason I want to say this is that the property right in a job does not apply to a person who is unable to get a job in the first place. But I believe that person has a right to a job.

Also, it seems plausible that the property right in one's job is vested, so to speak, over time—becoming stronger the longer one works at the job. This idea appears to be reflected in the standard union contract provision that distribution of layoffs be by inverse seniority, and in severance pay scales that are pegged to both rate of pay and number of years on the job.[17] This seems appropriate when weighing the claims of particular workers to particular jobs. But the worker with low seniority who keeps getting bumped off one job after another may put in many years of work without ever acquiring a strong property right of this sort in any job. Like the worker unable to get a job in the first place, the right of this worker to a job is not adequately represented as a property right in a particular job.

Moreover, it is, I think, commonly believed that if a property right is (legitimately) overridden, that right is adequately recognized, and its holder adequately compensated, if the full monetary value of the property is paid him or her. If this is correct, then if a (legitimate) plant shutdown results in a given worker becoming permanently unemployed (because unable to get another job) his or her property right in the lost job would be fully compensated if the appropriate proportion of projected earnings (up to 100 percent with sufficient years on the job) were replaced. This might be done by some combination of unemployment insurance, severance pay and early pension, adjusted over time to reflect as far as possible cost of living and wage increases that would have been received on the job.

There are at least two ways in which this wage replacement would not satisfy the worker's right to a job, even though it may well satisfy—or compensate for—the property right in the lost job. First, if the worker had been on the lost job only a short time, his or her property right (assuming that it is vested over time) would not amount to much. And if he or she is unable to find another job, this small amount does not compensate him or her for the opportunity to earn a living that the lost job represented. But if that amount is supplemented, say by welfare payments (justified by subsistence rights rather than job rights), so that the person has an adequate living, would there be any reason to say that his or her rights were not fully satisfied? I think there would, and this is the second way in which wage replacement would not satisfy the right to a job. Even a worker who receives 100 percent of projected income based on his or her property right in the lost job has a right to a job, a right which is not satisfied by wage replacement. Persons have a right to subsistence even if they cannot make a positive contribution to society. But they also have a right to make a positive contribution if they can.[18] The sense that one is making a contribution is a necessary condition of self-respect.

People need to feel that they are useful, productive members of society. This is not only a necessary condition of self-esteem and self-respect, but of mental and physical health generally.[19] Thomas Cottle, a sociologist and psychologist at Harvard Medical School, has studied the emotional impact of unemployment for fifteen years. He calls unemployment "a killer disease." "In our culture, working is close to the center of life. Our culture teaches that if you don't work in an acceptable way, then you're supposed to be depressed. And when job loss lasts . . . a million symptoms show—tooth decay, kidney failure, alcoholism, sexual infertility." Moreover, he says, the unemployed suffering mental health problems often do not seek help. "A lot of people want to go for help, but they don't want to bear the extra burden of feeling that along with being out of work, they're also crazy."[20]

Research by Dr. Harvey Brenner of Johns Hopkins University for the Joint Economic Committee of Congress showed that every long-term one percent increase in unemployment means: a 4.1 percent increase in suicides; a 3.4 percent increase in admissions to state mental hospitals; a 5.7 percent increase in homicides; a 4 percent increase in admissions to state prisons; and a 1.9 percent increase in deaths from cirrhosis of the liver resulting from alcoholism (Brenner, 1976, V). A recent study of workers affected by a plant shutdown revealed a suicide rate thirty times that of the general population (Cobb and Kasl, 1977).

Other studies have shown that unemployment is not only a source of psychological stress in itself, but also a cause of other stresses, such as having to move, becoming separated or divorced, all of which are correlated with higher rates of mental illness. Losing a job can set in motion a vicious cycle of other personal catastrophes that are much more difficult to handle for people who lack both the material and the emotional resources that a decent, stable job provides. Increased infant mortality and increased child abuse have also been linked to unemployment.[21]

It is, of course, likely that these effects would be ameliorated somewhat if loss of income did not accompany loss of one's job. But income, or other means of providing for subsistence (even at a fairly high level of material well-being) would not satisfy the need for a sense of oneself as a productive, contributing member of society. For most people in our society, that sense is inextricably tied to holding a job.[22] That is what it means to most of us to "pull our own weight." And it is this sense of oneself as a productive, contributing member of society that I claim is necessary for self-respect, self-esteem and mental and physical health generally.

It may be objected that people do not have a right to self-respect or self-esteem, or to mental and physical health generally. So how can the fact that a job is a necessary condition for these lead to a right to a job?

We do not have rights to these things because, important as they are, they are not things that other persons, or society as a whole, can provide or guarantee. But society can provide or guarantee some of the necessary conditions for them, such as adequate shelter and nutrition, a safe and healthy home and work environment, access to adequate health care (both preventive and interventionist), educational and other opportunities to develop knowledge and skills and undertake challenging tasks. To these, I claim, we do have rights. And, in our society at least, the right to a job is one of these rights.

These same considerations, moreover, lead to the conclusion that the right to a job must be understood, not as the right to just some job or other, however pointless, demeaning, and unchallenging, but the right to a job involving useful and challenging work.

In a paper discussing several studies of the mental health of workers in various kinds of jobs, psychologist Charles Hampden-Turner says:

> Perhaps the most detailed and perceptive study ever made of the condition of American workers was that of Arthur Kornhauser (1964) who studied Detroit automobile plants along with other smaller factories in the area. He used a measuring index of "Mental Health." Those with "Low" Mental Health typically suffered at least two psychosomatic symptoms. They had low self-esteem, periodic feelings of depression, poor social relationships, uncontrollable anxiety reactions, strong hostilities, chronic distrust, and poor life satisfaction. The absence of such symptoms, plus a positive feeling of self-worth and strong friendships, constituted "High" Mental Health. [Hampden-Turner, 1973, 33]

Only 34 percent of workers in large factories had high mental health (compared to 51 percent in small factories, 69 percent in nonfactory and 76 percent in white collar jobs). Moreover, the 34 percent with high mental health were mostly *skilled* workers, all with more than six years of steady employment and relatively secure seniority rights. The percentage of workers with high mental health correlated with job skill levels as follows: Skilled 58 percent; Semiskilled 35 percent; Repetitive semiskilled 10 percent; Repetitive, machine-paced, semiskilled 7 percent. Only those with very similar pre-job characteristics were used in making this comparison, so these differences cannot be attributed to social background or education.

Hampden-Turner also reports the conclusion of a paper reviewing seven studies of worker satisfaction and dissatisfaction: "Karsh concluded that satisfaction is bound up with the degree to which the worker can exercise his own judgment on his job and the extent to which he can control the conditions affecting his work" (Hampden-Turner, 1973, 39).

A special task force appointed in 1971 by the then Secretary of Health, Education and Welfare, Elliot Richardson, said in its report:

> We have sufficient evidence about the relationship between work and heart disease, longevity, mental illness and other health problems to warrant governmental action. That jobs can be made more satisfying and that this will lead to healthier and more productive workers and citizens is no longer in doubt. [*Work in America*, 1973, 114]

In a paper entitled "Meaningful Work" (1982), philosopher Adina Schwartz argues that commitment to an ideal of autonomy for all persons leads to the claim that no one should be employed in routine, repetitive jobs in which workers decide neither the overall goals of the enterprise nor how to perform their own jobs. She says that an individual achieves autonomy "to the extent that he/she rationally forms and acts on some overall conception of what he/she wants in life," and she argues that the empirical literature strongly supports the claim that autonomy, so understood, is undermined by such jobs. To achieve autonomy, people need to have opportunities to frame their own goals and decide how best to pursue them. Not having such opportunities at work undermines people's motivation and ability to be autonomous in the rest of their lives. She quotes Arthur Kornhauser in support of this claim:

> Factory employment, especially in routine production tasks, does give evidence of extinguishing workers' ambition, initiative, and purposeful direction towards life goals . . . [Kornhauser, 1965, 252]

> The unsatisfactory mental health of working people consists in no small measure of their dwarfed desires and deadened initiative, reduction of their goals and restriction of their efforts to a point where life is relatively empty and only half meaningful. [Kornhauser, 1965, 270]

It is, I think, significant that the same conclusion emerges from a commitment to the ideal of autonomy on the one hand, and from the more mundane-sounding commitment to guaranteeing, as far as possible, the necessary conditions for mental and physical health on the other. Schwartz's conception of autonomy includes, and goes beyond, self-determination, as I have been using the latter idea. As we have seen in this discussion and in earlier chapters, the right of self-determination both supports and is supported by health and safety rights. If, in addition, we are, or should be, committed to promoting autonomy, then we have another argument for the self-determination of workers in their work. It may not be an *independent* argument, however, for I suspect that something like Schwartz's conception will turn out to be the only plausible and coherent account of autonomy, and I further suspect that autonomy, so understood, is an important, perhaps the most important, aspect of mental health.

To sum up this part of the discussion, there are several ways in which health and safety rights and the right to a job are connected. The right to a safe job is empty if the cost of refusing an unsafe assignment is one's job. It is also empty if the cost of strong legal and/ or contractual health and safety provisions is a shutdown or run-away shop. The right to a job arises as a necessary condition for self-respect, self-esteem, and mental and physical health generally. The right to a useful and challenging job arises both as a necessary condition for mental and physical health and from the right to a safe and healthy job. Finally, a commitment to promoting autonomy also provides support for the right to useful and challenging work.

An exploration of the implications of the right to *useful* work would involve us in assessing *what* gets produced in our society and *why*. (Why are steelworkers and autoworkers, out of work as a result of plant closings or cutbacks, not employed in production to meet urgent human and social needs such as mass transit? Why are construction workers out of work when there is an urgent need for housing—both the renovation of existing stock and the building of new?) Exploring the right to *challenging* work would require us to look at *how* the work that is done is carried out, as we have begun to do here.

Four

The Case of J. P. Stevens

The issues raised by the case of J. P. Stevens include the right of workers to organize and bargain collectively, employer harassment of workers for attempting to exercise those rights, union security versus "right-to-work" laws, racial and sexual discrimination in the workplace, and the apparent inability or unwillingness of the courts and responsible agencies to protect the rights of workers under present laws and procedures. We round out our discussion with an examination of the right of public employees to strike and consideration of the right of union members to democratic participation in their union.

MAURINE HEDGEPETH: I went to work in the mill in 1957. Back in 1963 we started talkin' union. And we thought we had a right to do that. But we learned different. I testified at a National Labor Relations hearing in 1964. A few days later, I went on a pregnancy leave. On Christmas Eve they fired my husband, after him bein' a loom fixer for twenty-five years. In January, when my leave was up, they wouldn't give me my job back. We had three children and neither one of us had a job. They told us if any of us was goin' to get any work we would have to leave town to do it, because nobody here would hire us. I told them I would starve before I left town. . . . And we almost did. This is my home. My roots are here. . . . I don't like to think about the next four years. They were pretty hard years; when my kids asked for something to eat and I didn't have enough to feed everybody. And my children would say, "Mom, are you going to eat?" And I'd say, "I ate while I was cooking." You just don't forget things like that.

It took me four years and twenty-one days before I got my job back. I had to go all the way up through the courts. The Stevens Company had broken the law and had to put me back to work with full back pay. But nothing could make up for being out of work for four years and going without enough to eat.[1]

J. P. Stevens is the second largest company in the U.S. textile industry. It has annual sales of $1 billion and employs some 45,000 people in 85 plants, 63 of them in North and South Carolina. It is a multinational corporation with subsidiaries and associates in Canada, Mexico, France, Belgium, New Zealand and Australia.

In 1963 the Textile Workers Union of America (now part of the Amalgamated Clothing and Textile Workers Union) launched an organizing drive at twenty-one Stevens plants.

> The Company responded with a campaign of harassment and surveillance of pro-union workers, and dismissals of Union leaders. In every one of the 21 plants, workers were discharged for union activity. The leaders of the union movement were fired, and other workers were intimidated to prevent their joining. One procedure used was to post a list of the Union organizing members on a plant's bulletin board. Then, as members were fired, or frightened into quitting the Union, their names were publicly scratched off the list. [NCC, 1978, 13]

In August of 1974 the workers at Steven's seven plants in Roanoke Rapids, North Carolina, voted to be represented by the Textile Workers Union of America. Once employees elect a union to represent them, the employer is required by law to bargain in good faith with the union to attempt to arrive at a contract. More than three years later, in November of 1977, when there was still no contract (there was no contract until October of 1980), the Governing Board of the National Council of Churches (NCC) adopted a resolution supporting the union-initiated consumer boycott of J. P. Stevens products.[2] Setting forth the reasons for this decision, the resolution articulates most of the issues raised by the Stevens case that will be discussed in this chapter:

> —Since a determined effort to unionize the J. P. Stevens Company began in 1963 the Company has been repeatedly found in violation of the National Labor Relations Act (NLRA) by both the National Labor Relations Board (NLRB) and by the courts;
> —The J. P. Stevens Company, even while proclaiming its commitment to equal employment practices, has been found guilty by the U.S. District Court of violations of the Civil Rights Act of 1964 and of widespread racial and sexual discrimination at its plants in Roanoke Rapids and Stanley, North Carolina;
> —The J. P. Stevens Company, already found guilty by the Fifth Circuit Court of Appeals of failing to bargain in good faith at its Statesboro, Georgia plant, is currently charged by the National Labor Relations Board with failing to bargain in good faith with the Union at its plants in Roanoke Rapids, North Carolina, with the result that there is still no contract—despite the fact that years have passed since the workers voted in August, 1974, to be represented by the Union;

—After careful consideration, the Division of Church and Society Committee to Investigate the J. P. Stevens Question agrees with the Second Circuit Court of Appeals ruling in 1972 that

Respondents (Stevens) have flouted our prior decrees in many ways. . . . We regard this pattern of flagrantly contemptuous conduct most seriously. Our system of justice cannot survive if litigants are seized with the notion that they can ignore the lawful orders of a court simply because they disagree with them. In addition, the record here strongly justifies the inference that (Stevens) deliberately took their chances in ignoring our decrees because they thought it profitable for them to do so. . . .

The record shows that J. P. Stevens is content to respond to serious charges brought against it not with a genuine attempt to correct previous errors or crimes, but by using every legal means to delay a final judgment, and when it is found guilty by flouting the court's orders;
—The Amalgamated Clothing and Textile Workers Union, having pursued all legal avenues of recourse, and being mindful of the continued harassment, intimidation and discrimination suffered by J. P. Stevens workers, has called for a boycott of J. P. Stevens products as the only remaining means to force the Company to behave legally and morally within any reasonable length of time. [NCC, 1978, 1–2]

Textiles

Textile workers are exposed to hazardous chemicals used as flame retardants, anti-static agents, softeners, oil or water repellents, bleaches, wetting agents, finishers, and dyes. Cotton fibers may be contaminated with arsenic sprayed on the cotton when it was growing. Synthetic fibers may contain traces of chemicals used in their manufacture, such as formaldehyde, which is severely irritating and causes cancer in laboratory animals.

The machinery used in textile manufacturing is often extremely noisy and dangerous.[3] Noise is hazardous in at least three ways. It leads to permanent hearing loss with prolonged exposure. It is stressful, and job stress has been recognized as a serious health problem. It makes it difficult or impossible to communicate with co-workers, increasing both isolation and the likelihood of injury, since a shouted warning or other danger signal cannot be heard.

A unique hazard faced by workers in the textile industry is innocent-sounding cotton dust. Byssinosis, or brown lung disease, is caused by an allergy-like reaction to cotton dust. The initial stages of the disease have been called "Monday fever" because the reactions generally occur when the worker returns to the mill after a few days off. These reactions are like asthma attacks, with shortness of breath, severe air hunger, chest tightness, and a dry cough. The symptoms are caused by the narrowing of medium and small air tubes and the accumulation of thick mucus in the tubes. As exposure continues over months and years, the attacks last longer, until the victim has lung trouble all week long. Repeated exposure can lead to chronic inflammation of the air tubes, or chronic bronchitis. Obstruction of the air tubes causes back-pressure on the air sacs and rupture of their delicate walls, leading to emphysema (Stellman and Daum, 1973, 181–82). In the advanced stages, work in dusty environments becomes impossible, and often victims are too disabled to work at all. At least 35,000 American textile workers are disabled by brown lung disease.

This hazard has been the subject of an important recent Supreme Court decision. In June, 1981, the Court upheld a 1978 OSHA standard limiting the level of airborne cotton dust permitted in textile mills to 200 micrograms per cubic meter. The suit against the standard was filed by the American Textile Manufacturers Institute and twelve major textile companies. It claimed that the standard was too strict and that the health benefits to workers would not be sufficient to warrant the economic cost to the manufacturers of meeting the standard. The plaintiffs argued that the law requires OSHA to conduct a cost-benefit analysis to justify its proposed standards. The Court based its ruling on the wording of the 1970 OSH Act, which states that the Secretary of Labor "shall set the standard which most adequately assures, to the extent feasible . . . that no employee will suffer material impairment of health or functional capacity." In the majority opinion, Justice William Brennan wrote: "Congress itself defined the basic relationship between costs and benefits, by placing the 'benefit' of worker health above all other considerations save those making attainment of this 'benefit' unachievable."

The textile industry was established and for more than a century flourished in New England, along that region's many rivers and streams. Out of a long history of struggle came unionization of the workforce, so that by World War II the industry was among those considered largely organized.

In the years following World War II, however, the industry began moving to the South, particularly to states with so-called "right-to-work" laws. The reasons for this move were varied and intricately interrelated—changing technology (especially with respect to energy sources); antiquated capital stock; employer desires to be free of collective bargaining, the lure of relatively low wage levels, and vigorous campaigns by the Southern states to attract the industry through tax advantages and implied promises of a "union-free environment."[4]

As a consequence, unionized New England is today all but gone as a significant sector of textile production and employment. It is a commonplace today to think of the industry as "non-union," dominated by anti-union employers who through a variety of means have successfully fought off the ongoing attempt to re-establish collective bargaining as a working way of life for textile workers.

As we have seen in earlier chapters, the effective protection and exercise of most worker rights, including health and safety rights, depends in large measure on the presence in the workplace of a strong, effective union. Efforts by textile workers to enforce their health and safety rights and reduce the physical hazards they face on the job are made vastly more difficult by the fact that they do not have an *effective* right to organize and act collectively. In this chapter, therefore, we shall direct our attention to this latter problem.

Discussion

In the early nineteenth century in the United States, any sort of union activity was widely held by the courts (and by statute in a few states) to constitute criminal conspiracy punishable by fine or imprisonment or both. Not only was there no legal recognition or protection of a right to engage in concerted action and to organize for purposes of collective bargaining, such activities were held to be contrary to law. By mid-century, courts began taking the view that union activity was not, in itself, unlawful, but specific actions were illegal if either the aim or the method for attaining it were judged illegal. In deciding on the legality of aims and methods, courts generally held that only actions in pursuit of union member's self-interest, narrowly construed, was legitimate. This view was based on the common-law doctrine that pursuit of economic self-interest by normal business methods can justify harm done to the interests of others. Thus, acts of solidarity with other workers, such as sympathy strikes and secondary boycotts, as well as strikes to prevent the hiring of non-union workers, were held unlawful in most states. (Reynolds, 1961, 122).

From the 1880's to the 1930's, the foremost employer weapon against union activity—particularly striking and picketing—was the court injunction:

> The injunction was originally a court order designed to prevent threatened damages to property before they occurred, under circum-

stances in which later action would not provide an adequate remedy. How could this procedure be used to prevent peaceable strikes involving no damage to the physical property of the employer? Legal ingenuity soon found ways around this problem. It was held that a strike, even when it did not injure the employer's physical property, was certain to injure his "justifiable expectation of profit" from continuous operation of the business. By treating this expectation of profit as a kind of intangible property, it could be shown that *any* strike was injurious to property. The employer could also allege, and the judge was free to believe, that the strikers were threatening physical damage as well, even when it later turned out that there was no basis for the claim. [Reynolds, 1961, 123]

The injunctions were usually drawn in such sweeping terms that anyone supporting a strike in any way might be held guilty of a violation. Persons accused of violating an injunction were tried without jury for contempt of court, punishable by fine or imprisonment. Theoretically, there was a final stage of the process at which the judge decided either to vacate the injunction or make it permanent. In practice, the strike was usually won or lost before this took place. Attempts by Congress and by several state legislatures to curb what they perceived as blatant abuses of the injunction were largely ineffectual.[5]

Throughout this period, employers were free to fire employees for joining or attempting to organize a union. If employees struck, an employer could simply fire them all and hire replacements. Indeed, according to the doctrine of employment at will, "employers may dismiss their employees at will . . . for good cause, for no cause, or even for cause morally wrong, without being thereby guilty of legal wrong."[6] In addition an employer could require a prospective employee to sign a document stating that he or she was not a member of a union and would not become one, or have any dealings with any union while employed by the employer. Dubbed "yellow dog contracts" by union sympathizers, these coercive agreements were made unenforceable by the Norris-LaGuardia Act of 1932.

In 1935, Congress passed the Wagner Act, guaranteeing employees the right to engage in concerted activity, organize into trade unions, and bargain collectively for mutual aid and protection, and creating the National Labor Relations Board (NLRB) to enforce the rights guaranteed by the Act.[7] Five categories of anti-union activities on the part of employers are declared unfair labor practices and prohibited by the Act: (a) interference with, or restraint or coercion of, employees in the exercise of their rights under the Act; (b) domination of, interference with, or financial support of a labor organization (i.e., company unions); (c) discrimination to encourage or discourage union membership except where a closed or union shop was established by agreement with a majority of the employees (the closed shop was later made illegal by the Taft-Hartley Act, which also empowered the individual states to outlaw the union shop); (d) discrimination against any employee for filing charges or giving testimony under the Act; and (e) refusal to bargain with the legal representative of the employees.

The Wagner Act was upheld by the Supreme Court in 1937 in several cases, the most important of which was *National Labor Relations Board v. Jones and Laughlin Steel Company.* According to historian Joseph Rayback, "The Wagner Act and the Jones-Laughlin case climaxed a century-long struggle by labor for recognition of its right to organize and bargain collectively. Its previous theoretical rights on these points now became practical rights; all industry practices which transcended or thwarted the right to organize were outlawed. Labor, in short, had finally secured equality of position in the nation's economy." (Rayback, 1966, 345–46).

In 1980, more than 10,000 persons who had been illegally fired from their jobs for engaging in union activities were offered reinstatement as a result of complaints filed with the NLRB (NLRB, 1980, 13). Many such cases are never reported, and in many that are, the employer successfully claims that the person was fired for some other reason. In 1981, some 13,000 air traffic controllers were legally fired from their jobs for striking. Also in 1981, the Darlington Manufacturing case was finally closed. In September of 1956 workers at a Deering-Millikan textile plant in Darlington, South Carolina, had voted to join the Textile Workers Union of America (now ACTWU). In October, 1956 the plant was shut down. Twelve years later, in 1968, after an NLRB trial, at least two appeals to the NLRB, two to the U.S. Court of Appeals and one of the U.S. Supreme Court, Deering-Millikan began negotiations with the union to arrive at a back-pay settlement for the workers laid off in the illegal shutdown. Twelve years after that, in December of 1980, a settlement was announced. And in 1981, a quarter-century after the shutdown individual awards, ranging from $50 to $36,000, to the illegally fired workers were ready to be made. About a third of the 553 were deceased (NCC, 1978, 10; *Labor Update,* May 1981, 14).

The workers at J. P. Stevens plants in the case that opened this chapter had no effective recourse against the company's flagrant unfair labor practices. Although they had the legal right to strike, they didn't dare to.

> Because the J. P. Stevens Co. has other non-union plants to which it could shift production from the Roanoke Rapids plants, a strike by the Union workers at Roanoke Rapids would expose the loyal Union supporters to fierce economic hardships, with no corresponding hardship on the Company. These textile workers are among the poorest and lowest paid industrial workers in the nation. They have no economic resources to fall back upon, and would soon be forced by hunger to return to the mills. In any case, the Company could legally replace any worker who went on strike with a non-union applicant. The result would be pro-union workers on the street and anti-union workers in the plant. [NCC, 1978, 26]

Is it possible that Joseph Rayback was overly optimistic in proclaiming that, with the upholding of the Wagner Act by the Supreme Court, "labor had finally secured equality of position in the nation's economy," and that its previous theoretical rights concerning organizing and collective bargaining had then become practical rights?[8]

A full discussion of the position of labor in this country today and of the apparent inability or unwillingness of government to protect and enforce the legal rights of workers and their unions would require at least an entire book—and far more knowledge and understanding than this author possesses. We shall, however, attempt to identify and briefly explore some relevant factors, and the relations among them.

One important factor that emerged in the preceding chapter is the problem of plant closings and runaway shops. An adequate solution to this problem appears to require at least two different sorts of development: (a) legislation of the sort discussed in Chapter Three, placing some restrictions on the right of a company to shut down or move a plant and providing for the sustenance *and re-employment* of those who lose their jobs in shutdowns and lay-offs, and (b) much more active cooperation among unions, including unions of workers in different industries and in different countries. Such cooperation is essential if unions are to be able to respond to the ability of conglomerates and multinational corporations to shift capital out of one industry or country into another where conditions are more favorable and to "discipline" dissatisfied workers in one plant by shifting, or threatening to shift, production to another plant on the other side of town or of the world. A number of unions are making serious efforts to develop international cooperation—perhaps most notably, of the U.S. unions, the International Association of Machinists (IAM). Such efforts are hampered by practical barriers to communication such as linguistic and cultural differences and sheer physical distance which make it difficult and expensive to bring together significant numbers of people on a regular basis to share problems and ideas. Cooperative activity is also seriously hampered by legal barriers imposed on U.S. unions by the Taft-Hartley Act amendments to the Wagner Act. Let us now turn our attention, therefore, to the Taft-Hartley Act.

Ever since the Wagner Act was passed in 1935, employers have sought to destroy it. Initially, they ignored it, hoping that it would be struck down by the Supreme Court (Rayback, 1966, 343–46). After it was upheld, they repeatedly sought either its repeal or passage of new measures designed to eviscerate it.[9] In 1947, they got their chance. In 1946 the country experienced the largest strike-wave in its history, as workers attempted to make up the losses in real wages they had suffered due to wartime and postwar inflation. In September, 1946, real wages were lower than at any time since American entry into the war, while corporate profits were 20 percent higher than in the best of the highly profitable war years. Despite the fact that real wages were down and profits up, wage demands were blamed by the media for the continuing inflation, and unions were blamed for the disruption and inconvenience accompanying the strikes. A political consequence of the campaign against labor was the election in November, 1946, of a Republican Congress. (Rayback, 1966, 393–95).

At the same time, the red scare was fully kindled, with industry representatives fanning the flames and directing them against the labor movement:

> In 1947 the Chamber of Commerce published *Communists in the Government, The Facts and a Program,* blueprint for the charge that the New Deal [of which the Wagner Act was a part] was only a Communist conspiracy, destined to become the Bible and inspiration of Senator McCarthy. In the same year it published *Communists Within the Labor Movement, Facts and Countermeasures.* This was the first gun in the battle to pass the Taft-Hartley Act, which became law that same year. [Boyer and Morais, 1972, 345]

The Taft-Hartley Act was one of more than a hundred bills designed to constrain union activity that were considered by Congress in 1947. It consisted of a conglomeration of measures suggested by the National Association of Manufacturers to "correct" labor practices that employers considered unfavorable to their interests (Rayback, 1966, 397–98). Indeed, Representative Donald O'Toole of New York said, "The bill was written sentence by sentence, paragraph by paragraph, page by page, by the National Association of Manufacturers" (Boyer and Morais, 1972, 347).

Even in the anti-union climate of 1947, it was clear that workers would not relinquish the hard-won right to organize and act collectively. So employers had to go for second best and talk about "achieving a balance between business and labor for the promotion of industrial peace." What they did with the Taft-Hartley Act was to undermine the ability of workers effectively to act collectively through their unions by a) prohibiting acts of working-class solidarity, and b) allowing (indeed, encouraging) individual states to prohibit arrangements whereby unions sought to promote internal solidarity and financial stability. The first of these measures effectively isolated individual unions from the collective strength of the organized labor movement, forcing each union to rely heavily upon its internal resources.[10] The second was aimed directly at these internal resources. Where "right-to-work" laws at the state level prohibit the union shop, unions face an endless struggle, long after an initial organizing campaign has been won, to retain existing members and recruit new ones. This constant struggle, forced upon unions just to maintain certification and financial solvency, diverts the energy and resources of these unions from their primary goals, to negotiate "good" contracts and to police effectively those contracts, once negotiated. Not surprisingly, and not coincidentally, as a union's ability to "deliver the goods" declines as a consequence of these restrictions, the attractions of collective action also decline.

Description of the Taft-Hartley Act as anti-communist helped to silence opposition, since opponents feared that if they spoke out they would be labeled "reds" (Boyer and Morais, 1972, 347). The specifically anti-communist measure in the bill was a requirement that each official of a national or international union file an affidavit assuring the government that he was not affiliated with communism or with the Communist Party. Failure to comply would cause the union to lose the protection of the law. The non-communist affidavit was used as a weapon in the ideological fights within the labor movement as well as by the government and employers. Unions whose officials refused to sign the affidavits or which were charged with being communist-led were purged from the CIO (which had itself been expelled from the AFL more than ten years earlier on charges that it was a communist conspiracy). Eleven unions, comprising almost

1,000,000 members, were expelled—all of those named in the Chamber of Commerce pamphlet, *Communists in the Labor Movement* (Boyer and Morais, 1972, 350–65).[11] Five of these unions were driven out of existence; two merged very soon after the purge with unions which were affiliated with the American Federation of Labor; one merged with another of the expelled unions; one survived until the mid-1960's before merging with a previously hostile rival. Only two unions—the United Electrical Workers (UE) and the International Longshoremen and Warehousemen (ILWU)—successfully withstood both government and rival union attacks and are actively functioning today.

The affidavit requirement was repealed in 1959 by the Landrum Griffin Act and replaced by an outright prohibition against anyone who was or had been a member of the Communist Party within the previous five years holding union office or serving in any responsible position in a union. Violation was punishable by imprisonment of up to a year, fine of up to $10,000, or both. This measure was struck down as unconstitutional by the Supreme Court in 1965.

Some unions still have provisions in their constitutions barring communists from membership or holding office, or both. Such clauses lie dormant for the most part, and legal challenges to them have been upheld in the courts. But it is significant that they have not been repealed. To propose repeal might cast suspicion on the proponent, and there remain many persons within the labor movement who have yet to learn the main lesson of the McCarthy era, that red-baiting others does not protect one against being red-baited in turn. On the contrary, it simply contributes to a climate which makes everyone more likely to be attacked. Thus anti-communism remains a factor that undermines the strength and effectiveness of the labor movement both from without and from within.

Written as a series of amendments to the Wagner Act, Taft-Hartley carried over the list of employer unfair labor practices from the 1935 law and added a list of union unfair labor practices. Thus the Taft-Hartley Act formally acknowledges the right of workers to organize and act collectively, but it places substantial barriers in the way of their doing so effectively.

Prohibited as *union* unfair labor practices, among other things, are sympathy strikes or secondary boycotts. That is, it is illegal to engage in, or influence workers to engage in, a work stoppage to force an employer or self-employed person to cease using the products of, or doing business with, any other person. One of the potentially most effective forms of cooperation among unions is outlawed by this measure. During the boycott of J. P. Stevens products, for example, UAW members at a G. M. plant in Canada shut down the assembly line by refusing to install J. P. Stevens carpeting in the cars. In less than half a day the Stevens carpeting was gone from the plant.[12] Had U.S. auto workers (or garment workers, retail clerks, or any other workers) done the same thing, both they and the union involved in the primary action (ACTWU) would have been subject to harsh legal action. If such acts of solidarity had been feasible in this country, it is unlikely that Stevens would have defied the law and refused to bargain for as long as it did.

In addition, as we noted earlier, Taft-Hartley outlaws the closed shop and Section 14(b) permits individual states to outlaw the union shop and any other form of union security agreement. In a closed shop, a person had to be a member of the union before he or she could be hired into the shop. In a union shop, a person must join the union within a specified time after being hired. Other forms of union security are agency shop and maintenance-of-membership agreements. In agency shop, workers are not required to join the union that represents them, but they are required to pay an agency fee to the union for the collective bargaining, contract administration, and grievance handling services it performs on their behalf.[13] In maintenance-of-membership, there is no membership or agency fee requirement, but employees who are members of the union at the start of a contract, or who join while it is in effect, must remain in the union for the duration of that contract; and workers hired while a contract is in effect must join the union and remain members during the life of the contract. A shop where there is no form of union security agreement in effect is termed an open shop—although, in practice, it often is not "open" to union members or sympathizers.

Regaining the closed shop does not appear to be a live issue in the labor movement today, apparently because the difference between a closed shop and a union shop is not of great consequence to most unions in terms of the security each type of arrangement provides for a union or the fairness of each to union members.[14] In contrast, repeal of Section 14(b), the provision which permits individual states to prohibit any form of union security agreement is widely regarded as indispensable to enable unions to function. A union that has to spend most of its time and energy attempting to maintain its mere existence in a plant cannot function as effectively to protect and promote the rights and interests of its members as can one whose existence is reasonably secure.[15]

Defenders of Section 14(b) and proponents of so-called "right-to-work" laws argue that union security agreements constitute "compulsory unionism," violating the rights of the individual worker who might choose not to join (or remain in, or financially support) a union. The argument runs along the following lines: Just as they have the right voluntarily to join a union, workers have an equal right *not* to join. A worker should not be coerced into what ought to be a voluntary association with others. A union shop, or its several variations noted above, by definition is "compulsory" unionism, an enforced association without regard to the worker's own wishes. Thus, the worker under the typical union security arrangement must pay tribute for the "right to work." This is an intolerable position for any citizen of a free society to be placed in.

The extent to which workers themselves object to the allegedly onerous coerciveness of the union shop was severely overestimated by the creators of Taft-Hartley. The original 1947 Act included a ban on the union shop unless a majority of all eligible employees voted by secret ballot for this provision in a special election conducted by the NLRB *separately* from the ratification of the rest of the proposed contract. In the more than 20,000 union shop clause ratification votes held in the first year of Taft-Hartley, more than 98 percent of the clauses were approved, and more than 95 percent of those participating voted "yes." Small wonder that the requirement for a separate, secret poll on the union shop was soon repealed (Reynolds, 1961, 200–201).

Even if 99 percent of all workers favored the union shop, "right-to-work" proponents would say, that doesn't give them the right to coerce the one percent into joining against their will. In response to this objection, let us expand a bit on the above arguments.

Defenders of union security argue that the label "right-to-work" is misleading since such laws have nothing to do with reducing unemployment, with providing opportunities for employment, or enhancing job security. On the other hand, opponents of union security claim that being required to pay dues or agency shop fees constitutes being forced to pay for what should be a right of any citizen: the right to work. Hence the label. But note that there are many things to which we have a right which we nevertheless are—without inconsistency or injustice—required to pay for. What is objectionable about the requirement that the exercise or enforcement of a right be paid for is the implication that a person's enjoyment of a right may be contingent on her or his ability to pay. Requiring all who can to share equitably in the cost so that the right or its enforcement may be equally accorded to all has the *opposite* implication.

I do not mean to suggest that everyone must be equally in a position to exercise or enjoy every right. On the most extreme interpretation, that suggestion would be absurd. You and I equally have the right to travel to California for our vacations. However, if I spend all my vacation time and money on a trip to Florida while you save yours for a West Coast spree, then I am not equally in a position to exercise my right to go to California, even if we started out with the same amount of time and money for this year's vacation. Clearly there is nothing objectionable here. On the other hand, Smith and Jones also equally have the right to go to California. Smith inherited a fortune and has never worked at a job; he will be in a position to go to California even if he goes to Florida, the Riviera, Acapulco, and Monaco this year. Jones is a single mother of three who works two jobs to make ends meet; she can afford neither the time nor the money to go anywhere on vacation. If you told her that by moving to California she could get a better job, one which would pay her as much as she now makes at both jobs, she still would have no way to get herself and her family there (even if she were ready to risk giving up her inadequate but hard-to-get rent-controlled apartment and two paying jobs on your say-so). It is far less clear that there is nothing objectionable here. Nor is it clear that there is nothing objectionable in the contrast between you and Smith or me and Jones.[16] A case which clearly was objectionable was the poll tax, which made a person's exercise of the right to vote contingent on that person's ability to pay the tax.

I suspect that it would be impossible to come up with a clear and defensible theoretical basis for distinguishing between the objectionable and the unobjectionable cases, and that there is likely to be substantial disagreement over where the line should be drawn. I believe that the line is not fixed, but shifts (and should shift) depending upon other features of the situation. These other features, which cannot be enumerated in advance, and which may have various implications depending upon what other features occur in conjunction with them, will determine how central a role the right in question plays in the general socio-historical context in which the case arises and in the particular lives of the individuals concerned. But I digress: more on these matters in Chapter Five.

Perhaps the least controversial examples of services we have a right to and yet pay for are police and fire protection. Social security, education, and medical care are others. In some of these cases, such as police protection, OSHA and NLRB activities, it may be said that what we pay for is not a right but enforcement or protection of a right or rights, e.g., not to be assaulted, to organize into unions, etc. Insofar as we pay for these in the form of required payroll taxes, however, this is not a relevant distinction for the point at issue. Union dues and fees are paid for the enforcement of independently existing rights of workers (e.g., their rights under OSHA) and for the securing and enforcement of additional contractual rights. In that sense, then, neither payroll taxes nor union dues are payments *for the right to work.* And the latter are not more coercive under union security agreements than the former are for all employees.

Of course, some opponents of union security would also regard some or all of these other requirements as violative of individual rights. Libertarians, for example, consider most, if not all, income taxes to be equivalent to involuntary servitude, and view the social security and unemployment insurance systems as combining forced labor (insofar as they benefit others) and unjustifiable paternalism (insofar as they benefit the person required to participate).[17] This is not the place for a full-blown discussion and critique of libertarianism. Let us note, though, that libertarianism does not support any substantive or positive right to work. Libertarianism supports each individual's rights against interference by others. Thus it supports a person's right to work *if* she or he can get a job—and everyone else's right to let her or him starve if not. This is not a position that is very attractive to most people in our society today. But if we, as a society, are not willing to stand by and watch people starve,[18] then it seems appropriate and fair that all who can do so share in the expense of providing the necessary insurance for those who turn out to need it.

If society as a whole is going to provide, say, police and fire protection for those within its bounds, it is fair that all who are able share the cost of that protection. There are at least two kinds of reasons for not permitting some persons to avoid paying and to fend for themselves. First, it simply is not feasible, in practical terms, to provide such protection selectively. If the police stop a robbery in progress, would they check the victim's ID, and if it showed he or she was a nonpayer, excuse themselves and tell the robbers to carry on? Would firefighters check the annual receipts before responding to a fire? Second, even if it were, or were to become, feasible (it would take only a few seconds to punch up the payment record of a burning house on a computer), we might not be willing as a society to watch a house burn that is (or might be) full of people—even though the owner chose not to purchase fire protection.[19] If we are not, then either those who do pay must pay also for the protection of those who choose not to, or everyone who can pay must do so. There are undesirable features of either arrangement. The first seems unfair and the second seems to restrict individual choice. Communities with volunteer fire departments and rescue squads accept the unfairness of carrying the free-riders. Where people are willing and able to do this, one can regret the unfairness, but still regard it as an acceptable system, since those who bear the extra burden apparently do so voluntarily. Such a system is liable to be unstable, however. For if the numbers of those unwilling or unable to pay should increase (because of economic conditions, population growth, deterioration of a sense of community, or some combination of factors) to the point where some of those who had been sharing the burden become resentful of the free-riders and refuse to continue, and/or the contributions of those who pay become insufficient to cover the costs, the system may break down. If that should happen, or seriously threaten to happen, I maintain that the members of the community have a right to institute, by majority vote of themselves or their democratically elected representatives, a public firefighting or rescue squad system financed by mandatory tax payments. To deny them such a right would be to give to a few individuals the right, not just to opt out of the system, but effectively to prevent the majority from instituting a workable system to provide themselves with protection they want and need and have a right to. Thus, to say that the system of mandatory payment restricts individual choice is only part of the truth. To prohibit the institution of such a system also restricts individual choice—the choice of the majority of individuals.

Note that in the case of the voluntary fire department or rescue squad, everyone concerned has some interest in keeping the system going—at least up to the point where resentment or insufficiency of funds become serious problems. How much more unstable is a system of voluntary payment of the costs of union activity! From the very beginning, the employer has a strong incentive and many opportunities to encourage free-riders, and, to do whatever else can be done to destabilize the system so as to weaken and possibly eliminate the union. Thus, the breakdown of such a voluntary system is seriously threatened from the start. Why should not the community of workers have the right to institute by majority vote a system of mandatory payment of the costs required to protect their rights? It must be understood that under the present law they do not have that right even in the absence of state laws prohibiting union security agreements. The most they have is the right to negotiate, through their union, with the employer for inclusion of a union security clause in their contract. The state laws permitted under Section 14(b) of the

Taft-Hartley Act prohibit employers from contracting for such a clause with the duly elected majority representative of the employees.

Both proponents and opponents of union security see the issue as linked to that of exclusive representation. That is, the law provides that the union chosen by a majority of workers in a bargaining unit be the exclusive representative for all members of the unit rather than have any number of different associations representing groups of employees similarly situated and employed by the same employer, each negotiating separate contracts.[20] Because it is the exclusive representative of members of the bargaining unit, a majority union is required by law actively to represent every member of the unit whether or not he or she is a member of the union. The union must represent his or her interests at the bargaining table, enforce his or her rights under the contract, process grievances, go to arbitration and to court on his or her behalf, just as if he or she were a dues paying member of the union. Since these are very time-consuming and expensive activities, unions argue, it is unfair to require the union to undertake them unless those individuals can be required to pay a fair share of the cost.

Opponents of union security argue that the answer is to eliminate exclusive representation, which they say is more accurately described as "monopoly bargaining," and which they regard as, in itself, a form of compulsory unionism. The equitable solution, says Susan Staub of Concerned Educators Against Forced Unionism, a division of the National Right to Work Committee, is to let those who reject union membership fend for themselves. "Require unions to bargain only for those persons who *want* their services. After all, if a union is able to show its benefits to be attractive—if it does the best job—then teachers will want to join, and the so-called, 'free-rider' problem will be solved" (Staub, 1978).

Proponents of union security argue, first, that the law is correct in providing for exclusive representation. This is essential to permit effective promulgation and enforcement of the terms of a contract, and, most important, to prevent the employer from playing the different employee associations off against one another in the same way that, in the absence of a union, individual employees may be played off against one another. For this reason, too, individual contracts between bargaining unit members and the employer that are inconsistent with a valid collective bargaining agreement for that unit are not enforceable. Otherwise, an employer could easily break a union by giving nonmembers better contracts than union members,

thereby enticing members to leave the union and "fend for themselves." In such a situation, it would hardly appear that the union
was "doing the best job," since nonmembers would fare better than
members. Of course, once the union was eliminated, the bottom
would drop out, so to speak, for all the employees, and fending for
oneself would be a very different story. Thus Susan Staub's argument
ignores the ways in which the terms an individual is able to obtain for
him or herself depend crucially upon the context in which the
negotiations take place. There is no way the "independents" can
avoid benefiting from the presence of the union, and no way they
can, acting as independents, avoid weakening the union.

Unions in general accept the proposition that the duty of fair
representation—that is, the duty to represent all members of the
bargaining unit—is an appropriate corollary of exclusive representation. But, they argue, it is equally appropriate that all members of the
bargaining unit pay a fair share of the costs of fair representation,
even those who would prefer to "fend for themselves." Again, we
don't allow individuals to avoid paying their share of the police or
national defense or air pollution control budget on the grounds that
they prefer to go it alone. Why should this case be different?[21]

There is one more potentially serious argument against union
security that we must consider. Suppose a person is willing to join a
union but is denied membership (or is expelled) by the union. Where
union membership is a condition of continued employment, this
exclusion could cost a person her or his job (and conceivably even
make it difficult or impossible to get other jobs, especially in an
industry widely organized by the same union). If unions bar or expel
persons from membership because of such things as race, sex, sexual
orientation, age, political views, disagreement with union officials, or
personality, unjust and illegal discrimination in employment would
result. Thus if unions are to be treated as private, fraternal organizations which may select their members on any basis they choose, then
union membership must not be a condition of employment.

Agreed. There is no doubt that this has in the past been a serious
problem, especially with the closed shop. Some unions have had
discriminatory membership policies which effectively barred members of certain groups from employment in whole categories of jobs
and even in whole industries. As we have seen, the closed shop is
now outlawed, so the problem cannot arise in that particular form—a
form in which it would no doubt be very difficult to control. It is still a
potential problem with the union hiring hall, although, as we noted
earlier, it is unlawful for a union to discriminate in any of these ways

(or even on the basis of union membership itself) in its referrals. Because of the other pressing reasons in favor of the union hiring hall, and because there is no reason to believe job applicants would fare any better, in terms of discrimination, at the hands of employers, vigorous enforcement of the law prohibiting discrimination in referrals is probably the best available response to this problem.[22]

With regard to the union shop, as the law currently stands, if a union shop agreement is in effect, an employee may be discharged for failing to pay reasonable initiation fees and union dues after the probationary period. But under Section 8(a)(3) of the NLRA, "no employer can justify any discriminatory action against an employee for nonmembership in a union if it has reason to believe that membership in the union was not open to the employee on the same terms and conditions that apply to others, or if it has reason to believe that the employee was denied membership in the union for some reason other than failure to pay regular dues and initiation fees" ("A Guide to Basic Law and Procedures under the NLRA," 1978, 21-22). And it is an unfair labor practice for a union to cause an employer to discriminate against an employee in violation of Section 8(a)(3).[23]. Discrimination, then, does not seem to present any *special* problem in the context of union security agreements. It is immoral, illegal and exceedingly difficult to combat, but there does not appear to be any reason to think it is more difficult with union security than without it.

While we are on the subject of discrimination, it must be noted that racial, ethnic, and sexual prejudice and discrimination have themselves been important factors undermining the unity, and hence the strength and effectiveness of workers' attempts at concerted action. This is hardly a new point or a new phenomenon—although the particular forms it takes vary with time and circumstances. McLaurin, in his account of southern cotton mill workers and organized labor from 1875 to 1905, documents the ways in which mill owners encouraged and manipulated the exclusively white southern textile operatives' fear of being replaced by Negro labor during Reconstruction. He concludes, "Because of the white laborers' inability to overcome their racial prejudices, management was able to play the role of their protector against the blacks while, at the same time, using the blacks as a threat to keep wages depressed and hours of labor unchanged. Mill officials skillfully encouraged the mill hands' hatred of the Negro and manipulated that hatred to their own ends" (McLaurin, 1971, 65).

Similar tactics were used by J. P. Stevens to combat union organizing efforts there. A white woman worker in the documentary film, *Testimony*, reports: "Before the election they tried to pit the blacks against the whites and the whites against the blacks any way they could. They tried to make us think it was going to be a black union. But they were just trying to get the white people not to join the union." In this instance, the tactics were not successful.

But the problem is by no means a thing of the past. Indeed, the misperception that discrimination has been, not just halted, but reversed is today a major part of the problem. We cannot here discuss the many interconnected rights violations that are involved in or result from discrimination. For present purposes, though, it must be acknowledged that, to the extent that workers permit themselves to be divided by these issues, rather than devise constructive and equitable solutions, they cooperate in the defeat of their own attempts at effective collective action. The issue is divisive in large measure because groups of workers as well as individual workers are forced to compete with one another—in good times for decent jobs, in bad times for any jobs at all. But why must we accept the assumption that gains for minority and women workers must be achieved at the expense of other workers who are little or no better off than they? Why not insist instead that *all* who are able and willing to work have a right to decent, dignified, and meaningful jobs? (*That* would be a "right to work" worth supporting!) Of course, it is not easy and perhaps not always possible in specific concrete situations to translate this fine-sounding idea into achievable and acceptable programs and policies. But not to start from such a premise is to accept defeat from the beginning and to preclude the collective exercise of creative imagination that might give rise to proposed solutions that could unite rather than divide affected workers.

Our discussion so far in this chapter has been concerned largely with the rights of workers, as recognized and (however inadequately) protected under the National Labor Relations Act, to organize and join unions, bargain collectively, and strike.[24] Since, as we have noted, all public employees are excluded from coverage under the Act, our discussion would be seriously incomplete if it did not include some consideration of workers in the public sector: federal, state, county, and municipal employees. On the other hand, this topic is so enormously complex that we cannot hope to give it adequate treatment here. (A major source of complexity is that different statutes may apply in different municipalities within the same county or state as well as in different states within the nation. Moreover, where various units of government may or may not have enacted relevant statutes, the issue often becomes what rights public employees in a particular jurisdiction have in the absence of specific legislation.) We shall limit our consideration to the issue of the right of public employees to strike—which alone is sufficiently complex to preclude comprehensive treatment.

This issue is of great importance for at least three different reasons. First, the public sector employs a large and growing percentage of the paid labor force in the U.S., so rights denied public employees are denied to large numbers of workers.[25] It is thus quite misleading to assert that workers in this country are accorded certain rights if those rights do not extend to public employees. Second, the strike threat and the strike itself are, in practical terms, essential components of the collective bargaining process. Without these—or some *effective* substitute—an employer has precious little incentive to negotiate seriously or in good faith. Thus the substance of the right to bargain collectively is bound up with the right to strike. Third, it may be argued that the direct moral grounds for a right to strike are very strong. Indeed, given that, in an ordinary strike in the private sector, an employer is free permanently to replace striking workers, it seems but a few short steps from the right against involuntary servitude to the right to strike.[26] If you have a right to withhold your labor, you have the right to quit your job and the right to put your job on the line in negotiations with your employer. Since you also have the right (both morally and Constitutionally) to freedom of association, which provides the basis for the right to concerted action, it is hard to see how you can fail to have a right to strike (and hence also to threaten to strike). If this argument is sound with respect to workers in the private sector, a powerful reason is needed to block its application to the public sector as well.

With regard to the legal status of public employee strikes, there is a point that may require clarification. The statement that public employees in a particular jurisdiction do not legally have the right to strike can mean one of two different things. First, it can mean that such employees are prohibited by law from striking, as indeed all federal employees are by Section 305 of the Taft-Hartley Act. Second, it can mean that in that jurisdiction, for example, the state of New Jersey, there is no legislation specifically granting or recognizing the right of public employees to strike. In the former case, but not the latter, to strike is to break the law. Yet from the statement that public employees do not have the right to strike, where this is true in the latter sense, it is often erroneously concluded that public employee strikes are illegal. (This elementary mistake is frequently made by state officials when there is talk of a public employee strike in New Jersey, for example.) The practical effect of this difference tends to be short-lived, however, because the employer can seek an injunction to prevent or halt any threatened or actual strike, and, in the absence of legislation protecting the workers' right to strike, such an injunction is extremely likely to be granted. To go out or remain out on strike in violation of a court injunction is, of course, illegal, and strikers are subject to fines and imprisonment for contempt.

Let us now consider the main arguments advanced against the right of public employees to strike.[27] (In view of the clarification above, I should say that I shall understand arguments against the right to strike as supporting specific legislative prohibition, and arguments for the right as supporting specific legislative recognition.)

Perhaps the oldest argument—if it can be called an argument—is based on the doctrine of sovereignty. (This is the same doctrine urged in support of claims to governmental immunity to lawsuits by individuals, e.g., for negligence; hence, "the doctrine of sovereign immunity.")[28] As originally conceived, this doctrine was appealed to as justification for denying public employees not only the right to strike, but the right to bargain as well:

> What this position comes down to is that governmental power includes the power, through law, to fix the terms and conditions of government employment, that this power cannot be given or taken away or shared and that any organized effort to interfere with this power through a process such as collective bargaining is irreconcilable with the idea of sovereignty and is hence unlawful. [Hanslowe, 1967, 14–15]

Another formulation of the view is provided by Neil W. Chamberlain:

> In Hobbesian terms, government is identified as the sole possessor of final power, since it is responsive to the interests of all its constituents. To concede to any *special* interest group a right to bargain for terms which sovereignty believes contravenes the *public* interest is to deny the government's single responsibility. The government must remain in possession of the sole power to determine, on behalf of all, what shall be public policy. [Chamberlain, 1972, 13]

Applying the doctrine specifically to the right to strike, Herbert Hoover said in 1928 that "no government employee can strike against the government and thus against the whole people" (Aboud and Aboud, 1974, 3). And in 1947, Thomas Dewey stated that "a strike against government would be successful only if it could produce paralysis of government. This no people can permit and survive" (Aboud and Aboud, 1974, 3).

On the other side, Sterling Spero wrote in 1948:

When the state denies its own employees the right to strike merely because they are its employees, it defines ordinary labor disputes as attacks upon public authority and makes the use of drastic remedies, and even armed forces the only method for handling what otherwise might be simple employment relations. [Spero, 1948, 16]

Even if one accepts the doctrine of sovereign authority, it has been argued, it does not follow that collective bargaining or striking by public employees must be prohibited. Legislatures have often waived sovereign immunity in other areas of law. In most jurisdictions, individuals are now able to sue public bodies for negligence, for example. And since sovereignty refers to the people's will as expressed in legislative action, the concept does not preclude—indeed, it seems to require—that the people may, through their representatives, enact legislation authorizing government to engage in collective bargaining and permitting public employees to strike.

A related objection to the claim that sovereignty precludes strikes by public employees distinguishes between what might be called legal and political sovereignty. Legal sovereignty, according to this view, exists in order to meet the need for a peaceful, final, and enforceable means of settling disputes within society. Political sovereignty, on the other hand, refers to the process by which decisions are made in a political system. The American political process, it is pointed out, provides for no ultimate sovereign authority.

It might be added that the role attributed to government by the idea of legal sovereignty—that of a neutral or impartial third party for settling disputes—is clearly inappropriate where government itself is one of the parties to the dispute, e.g., as the employer in a labor-management dispute. This is so whatever one may think, in general, of the depiction of government as a neutral in disputes between private parties.

It has also been pointed out that the sovereignty argument as advanced by governmental units sounds suspiciously like the management prerogatives arguments private employers advanced against the rights of workers in the private sector to organize, bargain, and strike. If those arguments are properly rejected for the private sector, it is not clear why they should be accepted for the public sector. It is worth asking, moreover, what our reaction would be to the sovereignty argument if it were advanced by the government of another country as justification for prohibiting strikes by its citizen-employees. As the Executive Board of the Association of Federal, State, County, and Municipal Employees (AFSCME) has said, "Where one party at the bargaining table possesses all the power and authority, the bargaining process becomes no more than formalized petitioning" (Eisner and Sipser, 1970, 267).

A somewhat different version of the sovereignty argument relies on the claim that the public has rights, and these rights outweigh the right of public employees to strike. Hugh C. Hansen, for example, says:

> In a democracy, the people should decide what services the government will supply. The right to strike is a powerful weapon, subject to abuse, which would indirectly give workers the power to make those decisions. A public employee strike is only successful if it hurts the public. . . . The public has rights; it should not be reluctant to assert them. [Hansen, 1980]

This sort of appeal to the rights of the public, however, is subject to what seems to me a decisive objection. As Ronald Dworkin has argued, it eliminates the protection which recognition of individual rights is supposed to provide:

> It is true that we speak of the 'right' of society to do what it wants, but this cannot be a 'competing right' of the sort that may justify the invasion of a right against the Government. The existence of rights against the Government would be jeopardized if the Government were able to defeat such a right by appealing to the right of a democratic majority to work its will. A right against the Government must be a right to do something even when the majority thinks it would be wrong to do it, and even when the majority would be worse off for having it done. If we now say that society has a right to do whatever is in the general benefit, or the right to preserve whatever sort of environment the majority wishes to live in, and we mean that these are the sort of rights that provide justification for overruling any rights against the Government that may conflict, then we have annihilated the latter rights. [R. Dworkin, 1978, 194]

Thus, if we take seriously the claim that workers in general have a right to strike, we cannot justify abrogating that right by appeal to a conflicting right of the public to decide what services government will supply. (Note that Dworkin is not here objecting to the idea of group rights in contrast to that of individual rights; it is only the idea of the rights of society as a whole, or of a democratic majority, as potentially competing with the rights of individuals, corporations, or other corporate-like entities within the society, that threatens to annihilate the latter rights.)

If we reject the argument from sovereignty, then, there are two further arguments against the right of public employees to strike that pick up different threads from the arguments discussed so far. One appeals to preservation of the normal American political process, and the other to the essentiality of government services. The former may be dealt with more quickly, so let us consider it first.

> What sovereignty should mean in this field is not the location of ultimate authority—on that the critics are dead right—but the right of government, through its laws, to ensure the survival of the " 'normal' American political process." As hard as it may be for some to accept, strikes by public employees may, as a long run proposition, threaten that process. [Wellington and Winter, 1969, 1125–26]

But what is this normal political process? "Is something abnormal because it does not operate in conjunction with the standard political process and procedures of a particular era? Does the normal political process automatically exclude any methods or goals which will disrupt existing power relations?" (Aboud and Aboud, 1974, 4). And if a group "distorts" the political process by having more power than the average interest group, are public sector unions the only, or even the most salient examples? (Note that, by Dworkin's argument above, the "right of government . . . to ensure the survival" of the normal political process cannot be understood simply as a right to prevent individuals or groups from affecting and influencing the political process through the exercise of their rights.)

Is it true that recognizing the right of public employees to strike would give them such irresistible power that the political process would be seriously enough distorted to justify denying them that right? To argue that it would, it seems to me, one would have to base one's case on one or more independent reasons for thinking such disproportionate power would ensue. One of these—essentiality of government services—we shall examine next. Two others—absence of a competitive market in the public sector, and the idea that public employees have influence over their wages and working conditions through lobbying and voting—we shall consider briefly below.

The claim that government services are essential may be thought to provide support for prohibition of strikes by public employees in one or more of at least three ways. First, it may be argued that, since these services are essential, it is intolerable that they be interrupted, even temporarily, as they would be by a strike. A second argument is that if essential services *are* interrupted, the public will put enormous pressure on government to restore them, and government will have little choice but to cave in to union demands, no matter what they are.

Thus, if such strikes were permitted, public employee unions would be in an extraordinarily powerful position. Indeed, one opponent of the right to strike in the public sector likens public employee strikes to sieges or mass abductions because, in such a strike, an "indispensible element of the public welfare, be it general safety, health, economic survival, or a vital segment of cultural life such as public education, is made hostage by a numerically superior force and held, in effect, for ransom" (Saso, 1970, 37). A third argument is that, since government services are essential, the individual recipients of those services have a right to receive them. A strike that interrupted such services would, therefore, violate the rights of the would-be recipients, and, since the services are essential, the right to receive them must be an important right. These rights of individual recipients, then, may be said to compete with and outweigh any right of public employees to strike. (This appeal to the rights of individual members of the public does not run afoul of Dworkin's objection, above, which rejects only appeals to the rights of society, or the majority, as a whole.)

Clearly, however, not all government services are essential in the ways required for these arguments to be sound. In addition, somewhat different kinds and degrees of essentiality may be required by each of the three different arguments.

First, from the fact that a given service, such as public education, for example, is essential to society and its members over the long term, it by no means follows that any temporary interruption of such a service is intolerable. Public education is routinely interrupted for summer vacation, spring and fall breaks, holidays, and snow days. Time lost due to (legal or illegal) strikes by school employees can be, and is, made up by scheduling extra days and/or hours of classes. Are transportation services provided by municipal bus lines essential in ways that those provided by privately owned bus companies are not? If hospital workers in voluntary hospitals have the right to strike, why are public hospital employees different? Are their services any more essential? Upon reflection, it appears that few, if any, public services are essential in the way required to make the first argument sound, i.e., that even temporary interruption of them would be intolerable. Many who reject the first argument as applied to most government services do, nonetheless, accept it for two specific categories of service, those provided by police and firefighters. We shall return to these possibly special cases below.

In response to the second argument, that enormous public pressure to end a strike and restore services would force government to yield even to unreasonable union demands, there are at least three things to be said. First, in the absence of the economic pressure that a strike in the private sector exerts on the employer, public pressure to restore services is the only real leverage public employees can bring to bear on managment to come to terms. Striking workers, of course, forfeit wages and place their jobs on the line in the public sector just as in the private sector. So the pressure on workers to arrive at an agreement and end a strike is very strong indeed. In contrast, the public sector employer is likely to have tax revenues continue to accrue during a strike, while saving on the wage bill. Without public pressure for the restoration of services, management could comfortably wait out almost any strike, thus rendering the strike weapon totally ineffectual.

Second, the impact on tax rates of wage and benefit packages provides a strong incentive for public sector employers to bargain hard. "For the public employer, increases in the tax rate might mean political life or death; hence, unions are not likely to find him easy prey" (Aboud and Aboud, 1974, 6). And, as AFSCME's Victor Gotbaum points out:

> An automobile can increase in price 300 percent. Your food can go up 200 percent. If your taxes go up even less of a percentage, somehow the public is being raped by public employees. That is not so. In fact, our own studies show that the wage bill has not been going up that high since the arrival of unionism, taxes have not increased at a greater pace than costs in other areas, and yet we get this funny comparison that somehow when workers in the public sector strike, they get a helpless hopeless citizen. [Gotbaum, 1978, 161]

A third response to the second argument is that it is essential to identify the source of the public pressure. As Ronald Dworkin's argument above establishes, public disapproval or displeasure at being inconvenienced or made somewhat worse off does not justify the abrogation of a right. Certainly, then, the anticipation of public pressure arising from such displeasure cannot justify the abrogation of the right to strike. Thus it seems that prohibition of public sector strikes could be justified only by showing that they constitute a very direct and serious threat to the public safety or wellbeing, or that exercise by public employees of the right to strike would somehow violate more important rights of other members of society, as the third argument from essentiality of government services maintains. The claim that *any* strike would seriously and directly threaten the public safety or wellbeing does not seem at all plausible applied across the board to public employees. Again, it appears most plausible in the case of police and firefighters, although even here a blanket prohibition may be far more restrictive than is justifiable. We shall return to this question below.

Now let us consider the third argument, that the individual recipients of government services have rights to those services which would be violated if they were interrupted by a strike. First, from the fact that an individual has a right to a government service it does not follow that the right is violated if the service is temporarily interrupted. Even a very important right to a given service need not be violated by a temporary interruption, as it would be, let us suppose, by permanent cessation of the service. Moreover, from the fact that individuals have very important rights to certain services it does not follow that the onus is entirely upon government workers to provide those services without interruption under whatever conditions management chooses to impose. The right is against government or society as a whole, whose obligation it is to create and maintain conditions in which qualified workers are willing to work and provide those services.

It is worth noting, too, that in many instances the issues over which government employees are likely to strike are issues on which the interests of the recipients of government services coincide with those of the providers. Welfare workers demanding lighter case loads, teachers insisting on smaller classes, air traffic controllers complaining about obsolete equipment, understaffing, and compulsory overtime are all instances of government workers attempting to secure adequate conditions in which to do their jobs. The rights of the recipients of these services are not protected by prohibiting the providers from using what may be the only effective means of securing such conditions—quite the contrary. Even where this is not the case, there appear to be no grounds for a general claim that strikes by public employees would violate the rights of the recipients of governmental services. If such a case is to be made, it must be made in much more particular terms with respect to specific categories of service. Once again, the chief candidates presumably will be policing and firefighting, to be discussed below.

Let us now briefly consider two additional reasons which have been offered in support of the claim that recognizing the right of public employees to strike would give them such power as to seriously distort the political process: absence of a competitive market in the public sector, and the claim that public employees have the opportunity to influence their wages and working conditions through lobbying and voting.

The absence of competitive market forces in the public sector has been said to lend disproportionate power to striking public employees in two ways. First, it is argued that in the private sector market forces such as elasticity of demand for the employer's product and the extent of nonunion competition limit the ability of an employer to absorb increased labor costs. Since employees recognize these limits, and have no interest in putting the employer out of business, they have reason to limit their demands accordingly. In the absence of such forces, it is held, public employee unions have little reason to restrict their demands to reasonable levels. This argument seems to ignore the fact that all striking workers have a very direct incentive to reach a settlement—they lose wages each day that they are out. Even with a strike fund, strikers' incomes are drastically reduced, and in a prolonged strike, any existing strike fund is in danger of being exhausted. Moreover, unions in the public sector are not entirely insulated from competitive labor. The threat of permanent job loss through layoffs or even complete elimination of public agencies is very real. Santa Monica, California, for example, ended a strike of city employees by threatening to contract out its sanitation work. In Warren, Michigan, a similar threat was carried out (Burton and Krider, 1972, 277).

The second way in which the absence of market forces is said to result in greatly increased power for potential or actual strikers in the public sector is that public employers, not needing to minimize costs to remain competitive and profitable, will not bargain hard. As we saw above, however, the pressure to keep tax rates down can also provide an effective incentive for hard bargaining. Indeed, in many cases, the absence of a competitive market can work to strengthen the hand of the employer rather than that of the union, since the economic pressure a private sector strike brings to bear on the employer is absent, or greatly reduced, in the public sector.

Our final candidate for an argument showing that granting public employees the right to strike would seriously distort the political process is the claim that, unlike private sector workers, public employees and their unions have the opportunity to affect their wages and working conditions through the political process, so that if they had the right to strike as well, they would wield undue power. Thus it has been argued that, through collective bargaining, public employee unions can acquire the maximum concessions management will offer at the bargaining table, and then they can apply political pressure, through lobbying efforts and voting strength, to obtain additional concessions. If the right to strike were added, according to this argument, public sector bargaining would be heavily weighted in favor of employees.

But the capacity of public employee unions to influence legislative decisionmaking is a necessary (and often inadequate) counterweight to the tendency of legislators, responding to public pressure to keep taxes down, to solve difficult and ubiquitous fiscal problems at the expense of public employees. Representatives of each of the different categories of government workers must attempt to bring their concerns to the attention of legislators in an effort to avoid being lost in the budgetary shuffle. Further, although they constitute a growing percentage of the workforce, public employees as a group are unlikely to constitute anything approaching a voting majority in any given jurisdiction. And, although public employees as a group may constitute a potentially significant voting block, those workers directly affected by negotiations over any particular contract will almost certainly be a tiny minority. Thus, whatever truth there may be to this argument, it seems grossly inadequate to the task of showing that if on top of their right as citizens to participate in the political process they had, as workers, the right to strike, the political process would be so seriously distorted as to justify prohibiting the exercise of one of these important rights.

We have been unable to find any justification for a general prohibition of strikes by public employees. I conclude that public employees generally, like workers in the private sector, have the moral right to strike, and that right ought to be recognized and protected by law, as it is for all other workers.

We must turn now to consider whether police and firefighters constitute a special case where prohibition of strikes may be justified, even though it is not justified for other public employees. We shall not be able to give this complex and admittedly difficult question adequate discussion here, but we can try at least to identify some of the relevant considerations.

Of the various arguments discussed above, only those appealing to essentiality of services may apply differently to police and firefighters than to other public employees, so those are the only arguments relevant here. As you may recall, there were three arguments from essentiality of services. First, it may be argued that police and firefighting services are essential in a way that makes it intolerable for them to be interrupted, even temporarily. The second argument claims that, if such services were interrupted by a strike, public pressure to have them restored would be so strong that even outrageous demands would be agreed to. Thus police and firefighters are in a position to "hold hostage" the public safety. And, third, individual members of the public may be said to have very important rights to the protection of their lives, safety, and property that police and firefighters provide, rights that would be violated if those protections were suspended by a strike.

Concerning the second argument, the burden of proof must be on those who would deny an important right to show that there is more than a theoretical possibility that the right would be abused in seriously harmful ways. More than that, many of our important rights and freedoms are occasionally abused in ways that result in serious harm to others. In most cases, we reluctantly accept the risks in order to preserve the freedoms. Proponents of prohibition of strikes by police and firefighters must, then, provide convincing evidence that legal recognition of their right to strike would create a serious *practical* threat that is out of proportion to the other risks we endure out of respect for rights. I have so far seen no reason to believe that such evidence can be produced. Note, too, that the fact that the restriction in question applies to a minority of the members of society, in contrast to many other possible restrictions of rights that might be adopted, is a reason to be suspicious of it.

Let us grant, though, that one or more of these arguments may have some force in the case of police and firefighters. Is that force sufficient to justify flatly denying to these individuals an important right? The answer to this question seems to depend on what the available alternatives are. It may be that, with some constraints, the right to strike could be retained by these workers without serious threat to the rights or safety of the public. If so, outright prohibition of such strikes still would not be justified.

For example, provision might be made for partial work stoppages with emergency services continued for life-threatening situations. Police functions include many that could be interrupted with some inconvenience but little serious danger to the public; for example, traffic control, parking violations, paper work not immediately essential to protecting the rights either of victims of crime or of the accused. Firefighters might respond to alarms but limit their firefighting to those measures needed in order to carry out all possible rescue efforts.

Another possibility is to provide for a mandatory "cooling off" period of, say, thirty or sixty days. This could be either automatic or available to be invoked by the appropriate public official if he or she deemed it necessary. During this period, mediation could take place in an effort to help the parties reach voluntary agreement. (A mediator is a third party who attempts to help the disputants find a resolution they can agree upon. A mediator has no power to impose a settlement.) Also, during such a period, public officials would have the opportunity to make contingency plans for protecting the public in the event of a strike. It may be objected with some justification that such a "cooling off" period is, or should be, unnecessary. Mediation efforts could be undertaken before, rather than after, a contract runs out, and contingency plans could be made when officials see that negotiations are not going well and the contract is within a month or two of running out. Nevertheless, supposing that public officials sometimes lack wisdom and foresight, and that the public safety may be at stake as a result, there may be some grounds for such a provision.

I see no reason why some such constraints would not suffice to eliminate any serious special threat to the rights and safety of the public that the prospect of a strike by police or firefighters poses. But since some will no doubt remain unpersuaded, and since the precise nature and degree of constraints justifiable on these grounds will be controversial among those who are persuaded, it may be worthwhile to look briefly at what the alternative is if the right to strike is entirely denied. Some procedure must be provided for arriving at a settlement when contract negotiations are at an impasse.

The principal alternative is compulsory binding arbitration. Arbitration differs from mediation in that an arbitrator investigates a dispute and issues a decision which is binding on the parties.[29] There are two sorts of labor disputes in which arbitration may be used. It is most commonly used as a final step for resolving individual grievances that arise under an existing contract. Frequently, the contract itself provides that grievances that are not resolved by the other measures provided in the grievance procedure will go to arbitration. The second kind of dispute is that in question here, where the parties are unable to reach agreement on a contract. We shall be discussing only arbitration of the latter sort.

In the most usual form of arbitration for settling the terms of a contract, the parties present and argue for their positions on the issues that are in dispute, and then the arbitrator draws up terms that he or she considers most fair. Thus the arbitrator may impose terms that were not proposed by either party. It has been objected against this sort of arbitration that, since arbitrators most often "split the difference" between the two sides, there is little incentive for the parties to bargain in good faith, since the more extreme the position they present to the arbitrator the more they are likely to get in the compromise.

To avoid this problem, another form of arbitration has been proposed. It is called final-offer arbitration because the arbitrator is restricted to a choice between the final offers of the two parties on all unresolved issues. The arbitrator may not pick and choose among the offers of the parties on different issues—the choice is between one total package or the other. The purpose of this restriction is to provide a strong incentive for each party to make the most reasonable possible proposals—with the hope that, in so doing, they may even arrive at an agreement without going to arbitration. A serious problem with this procedure is that one or both of the final offers may contain some provisions which are eminently reasonable and others which are not. An employer's final offer, for example, might be very reasonable in terms of wages and benefits, but contain a change in the grievance procedure that would be disastrous for the union. In addition, an arbitrator, who is not familiar with the day-to-day operations and problems, may not be in a position accurately to assess which proposals—especially non-economic proposals—are reasonable.

This latter problem constitutes an objection against compulsory arbitration in any form. The parties themselves know best what the issues mean in terms of what it would be like to live and work under a given provision for the next year, two years, or three years, depending on the duration of the prospective contract. They know which issues are so important to them that they are worth risking a strike over, and which provisions they can live with. No third party can know these things as well as the disputants themselves. Thus, both practical considerations and appeal to the right of self-determination argue in favor of allowing the parties to settle their disputes themselves, even if that means strikes will sometimes occur.

Another potential problem with final-offer arbitration is that a different form of "splitting the difference" would tend to arise. Since both parties generally have the right to veto the appointment of an individual arbitrator—and surely they must have this right, since this individual will determine the terms and conditions that will govern their working lives for, typically, one to three years—there will be a strong tendency for arbitrators to decide half of their cases in favor of management and half in favor of unions. An arbitrator with a record of decisions going too often either way would soon be out of work. Now it may be thought that this pressure should be welcomed, since it amounts to a strong incentive for arbitrators to be even-handed, and hence fair. But it must be noted that there is little reason to expect that, over any given period of time, for any particular arbitrator, management will have made the most reasonable offer in just 50 percent of the cases he or she hears, and the union in the other 50 percent. Yet the pressure is to build a record that appears to reflect just this situation.

Finally, whichever form of arbitration is used, some opponents of compulsory arbitration argue—with a good deal of plausibility, in my view—that arbitrators tend to have backgrounds, educations, lifestyles, and social contacts that lead them, consciously or unconsciously, to identify more with supervisors, managers, and public officials than with workers. This identification cannot help but influence their sympathies, their assessment of the arguments put forward by the parties, and hence, ultimately, their decisions. Thus, a system of compulsory arbitration is, probably inevitably, biased in favor of management and against workers. Note that this objection is compatible with the previous one, although it may at first appear not to be. If unions are aware of the pro-management bias of arbitrators then they will risk going to arbitration only when their case is particularly strong. They will settle voluntarily in many cases where they ought to win in arbitration but probably would not. In such a situation, unions would have a better case than management in significantly more than 50 percent of the cases that actually got to arbitration, so a fifty-fifty split of the decisions would reflect a promanagement bias.

For all of these reasons, then, compulsory binding arbitration is unsatisfactory as a substitute for the right to strike. As a matter of political reality, however, it may be that, given the kinds and degrees of constraint likely to be placed on their right to strike by legislators in a given jurisdiction, police and firefighters do better to accept a system of arbitration than to retain a right to strike that would be rendered utterly ineffectual.

To conclude this discussion of the right of public employees to strike, it must be emphasized that prohibition of strikes does not prevent strikes. Indeed, it can be argued that it is likely to have the opposite effect. New Jersey's Commissioner of Labor and Industry said in 1965 that "it may be more critical to have the strike weapon available to workers to alert management, government, the customers of the government, and the public that they must do something; they cannot go on ignoring the problem" (Male, 1965, 109). (As we noted above, New Jersey still has not recognized the right of public employees to strike.) Allan Weisenfeld develops the argument as follows:

> Strikes in the public sector will be no more frequent, probably less, than in the private sector and cause no greater inconvenience and disloca-

tion. . . . It is the denial of the right to strike in the public sector . . . which invites strike threats. Anti-strike laws create a tendency on the part of public managers to rely on them to bail them out, and hence, they tend to contribute little to help solve the problems before the bargainers. [Weisenfeld, 1969, 139].

Prohibition of strikes may thus exacerbate the very problems it is intended to solve.

Toward the end of Chapter Three, we explored some considerations that support the claim that, in our society, everyone who is willing and able to work has a right to a job. We noted that many of the same considerations suggest that such a right should be understood, not as a right to any job, however meaningless or degrading, but a right to challenging and useful work. There we explored briefly the relations among the right to participate in decisions importantly affecting one's life, the right of self-determination, and the right to autonomy. We saw how the first and second, arising from the practical day-to-day need to protect one's life and health, constitute an important component, possibly the central core, of the third. So the ideal conception of a person that is represented by the notion of autonomy both supports and is supported by the more tangible idea of participation in decisions that affect one—with the idea of self-determination mediating between the two.

Let us now add that many of these same considerations, and others as well, support every union member's right to democratic participation in the affairs of his or her union, from the shop floor to the office of the national or international headquarters.[30] Many of the more particular rights comprising the general right of democratic participation in one's union are legally established by the Labor-Management Reporting and Disclosure Act of 1959, as Amended (LMRDA), often called the Landrum-Griffin Act. This law provides for such things as equal rights for all members, freedom of speech and assembly (right of members to speak out on all union affairs and criticize the conduct of officers and to form caucuses or otherwise associate with others inside or outside the union), the right to due process in any disciplinary action taken by the union, rights of access to information about the union's constitution, finances, and officers, and the right to a copy of the collective bargaining agreement for one's bargaining unit. It also provides for the right of all members to vote on proposed dues increases and in elections for higher level union officers. Members do *not*, however, have the (legal) right to vote on any other issue, including the ratification of their own contracts, unless that right is provided by the union's constitution. Because the contract they work under affects their lives in direct and important ways, many members of unions that do not have contract ratification by the membership are justifiably critical of the absence of what seems a basic democratic right.

If it were practically feasible to protect the rights of workers by negotiating contracts, getting laws passed, and filing complaints in court or with government agencies in the event of violations, then it might at least appear that all this could be handled by a union's higher officials and their professional staff. It would appear as if a union could effectively *represent* and *act on behalf of* its members even though it would be false—or only *formally* true—that the union *was* its members. In my view, this appearance would be deceptive even in the hypothetical circumstances described, but it would have some initial plausibility.

The more evident it becomes that government is unwilling or unable to enforce even the narrowly constrained rights to organize and engage in concerted action that it guarantees by law, the more apparent is the practical need for active participation by the rank and file. Even if things go smoothly for a period, so that an active and involved membership does not appear to be needed, when a crisis does occur a union's greatest strength is in the actual or potential collective action of a solidly united membership. This cannot be turned on and off at a moment's notice. People learn to participate by participating; they become informed about issues in large part by participating in decisions concerning them; if they are accustomed to participating, they often want and expect to participate more.[31] Thus, democratic participation is not only a matter of the rights of workers in their unions. It is also a necessary condition for the effective functioning of unions to protect the other rights of workers.

Five

Rights

It is time now to become a bit more abstract and discuss directly the concept of rights which we have largely taken for granted in the preceding chapters. In this chapter we sketch the rough outlines of an account of the nature, origins, functions, and limits of rights.

It would be grossly out of proportion to call this brief sketch a theory of rights. To present a full theory—if one had one—would require at least an entire book devoted to that project alone. Still, any book which relies as heavily as this one does on arguments to and from various claims about rights owes to its readers some account of what is to be understood by such talk of rights. This chapter is, in large measure, an attempt to make good that debt. In somewhat smaller, though not inconsiderable measure, the first four chapters of this book are an attempt to develop the sort of practical, contextual basis that, in my view, must inform any adequate moral and political theory, including a theory of rights. To that extent, this chapter is an attempt to point in the direction that an adequate theory of rights must take. (I do not mean to suggest that others have not struck out in this direction before.)[1]

Many different schemes for classifying various purported kinds or categories of rights have been proposed by philosophers and legal theorists over the years. Different sets of terms have been used to draw often similar but seldom identical distinctions; some systems of classification cut in entirely different directions from others; sometimes different terms used for what appear to be the same sort of rights reflect different background beliefs about their origin or range of application. It would be a long and tedious, though perhaps illuminating exercise systematically to lay out, discuss, and compare even the best known and most influential of these schemes. I shall attempt nothing of the kind here. A few preliminary remarks, however, do seem in order.

I am concerned with both moral and legal rights, and with the relations between them. I take it that some—indeed, a great many—rights are both moral and legal. When I speak of a right without further specification, I mean at least a moral right, which may or may not also be a legal right (whether it is or not should, if revelant, be clear from the context). Still, there are some moral rights that are not recognized in law and others that are recognized only inadequately or incompletely. There are some legal rights that correspond to no moral rights and some that are more extensive than the moral rights to which they are thought to correspond. And the legitimate expectations created by the existence of some legal rights may create moral rights where none would otherwise have existed.

I do not speak of "natural rights" or of "human rights" for two reasons. One is that both terms—the first perhaps more than the second—suggest that persons have rights independently of social institutions, solely in virtue of being human. I reject this view. The second reason is that these terms are often used to distinguish some rights, thought to be held "naturally" by all humans, from others thought to arise only in certain social contexts. Since I do not believe there are rights of the first kind, any distinction of this sort must, on my view, be one of degree. Some rights, such as the right to minimal means of subsistence and the right not to be tortured, apply wherever there are rights at all. Others, such as A's right that B pay her ten dollars, arise only in special institutional contexts of lending, trading, betting, and so on, and only as a result of relations in which the parties stand to each other within those contexts.

Categories of rights, such as workers' rights or the rights of aliens, on this view, are not special kinds of rights, but ones which arise out of the needs, problems, and predicaments that face persons in a certain kind—or perhaps a fairly broad range of kinds—of situation. Thus some such rights will be particular to the role or situation in question, while others will be rights persons also have in other areas of life. The right to bargain collectively, for example, or to strike, would have no application in, say, a family subsistence peasant economy. But when a multi-national corporation moves in and begins employing some of the local people, such rights become applicable, even if they are not recognized in the laws of the country, or by the people employed. Other rights, such as health and safety rights, free speech rights, and the right to due process, have application both in the workplace and outside it, though the particular forms they take may be different. (The application of some of these rights to workers, as workers, is not yet legally established in the U.S. Workers do not, unless provided by union contract, have legally enforceable due process or free speech rights on the shop floor, for example.) Often specific rights that apply to a particular kind of role or situation will be relatable to other, more general rights, and perhaps derivative from them. We should not, however, expect to be able to construct a neat hierarchy or system of rights, all deriving from some small set of general human rights.

I take moral rights to include rights that individuals, corporate entities, classes, communities, political units, or the moral community as a whole may hold against other individuals, corporate entities, classes, communities, political units, or the moral community as a whole, in almost any combination. Thus, not only individuals can hold rights, although, due to the individualistic character of the sort of world and world-view which give rise to rights, there is some tension in the idea of a right being held by other than an individual person.

But what are these moral rights, and do they really exist? Rights are social relations. This is reflected in the fact that full specification of a right requires identification of both the right holder and the person(s) or agency against whom the right is held. A right against one person or agency may give rise to a right against another, as when I have a right against you that you turn over the car I have paid you for, and a right against the government that it enforce my right against you. Or it may not, as when I have a right against you that you keep your promise to help me move, but no right against the government that it enforce this right. Now human society—and indeed human life itself—without social relations is impossible, so that the existence of social relations is a fixed condition of human life and society. But the particular form and nature of those relations can—indeed must— change as the other circumstances of life change. That does not mean the social relations are not real.

Of course, social relations are not *entities*, and there is often a temptation to think that only entities are real. But on reflection it does not seem reasonable to affirm the reality of entities while denying the reality of the qualities and activities of, changes in, and relations among, those entities. What could it mean to say that things are real but none of their attributes are real?

Social relations, then, are as real as the individuals, groups, and institutions that participate in them. And, on my view, the nature of individuals, groups, and institutions is at least as much constituted by the social relations in which they engage as the nature of the relations is by the individuals, groups, and institutions engaged in them.[2]

Thus, I believe that moral rights are real, that is, that people have them. And I believe they are extremely important. Unlike some who share these beliefs, however, I do not take any rights to be inborn, universal, or unchangeable.

Rights are a fairly recent development in human history. They evolved in the course of the transition from the rigid hierarchical economic-political structure of feudalism, in which one's station with its powers and duties was determined at birth, to the competitive individualistic system of market capitalism (and the simultaneously evolving nation-state). This at least is when the concept and language or rights developed.[3]

Some would say that rights had existed all along, even though people previously had not recognized them. I should say rather that they came into existence along with a way of life to which they are appropriate, and in the context of which they are indispensable. This way of life is itself not fixed, and the conflicting tendencies and pressures that arise in the course of its continuing evolution manifest themselves, among other ways, in disputes over the nature and significance of rights.

Many such disputes may be characterized as variants or close relatives of disagreements over two different and sometimes competing conceptions of rights, one "negative" and the other "positive." Isaiah Berlin developed this positive-negative distinction in his influential essay, "Two Concepts of Liberty" (Berlin, 1958). As the title indicates, his focus was on the concept of liberty or freedom, not that of rights. But the positive-negative contrast has frequently been applied to rights. And, of course, if a right to liberty is claimed, the content of that right will depend on whether liberty is understood in the positive or negative sense. The negative sense, according to Berlin, "is involved in the answer to the question 'What is the area within which the subject—a person or group of persons—is or should be left to do or be what he is able to do or be, without interference by other persons?' " The positive sense "is involved in the answer to the question 'What, or who, is the source of control or interference that can determine someone to do, or be, this rather than that?' " (Berlin, 1958, 84). The negative conception is expressed by the phrase "freedom from"; the positive conception by the phrase "freedom to" (Berlin, 1958, 91).

As Berlin points out, the negative notion of liberty is compatible with the absence of self-government:

> Liberty in this sense is principally concerned with the area of control, not with its source. Just as a democracy may, in fact, deprive the individual citizen of a great many liberties which he might have in some

other form of society, so it is perfectly conceivable that a liberal-minded despot would allow his subjects a large measure of personal freedom. . . . [T]here is no necessary connexion between individual liberty and democratic rule. The answer to the question 'Who governs me?' is logically distinct from the question 'How far does government interfere with me?' It is in this difference that the great contrast between the two concepts of negative and positive liberty, in the end, consists. [Berlin, 1958, 90]

Of course, taking a right to either negative or positive liberty as primary, one might argue that it supports a derivative right to the other. Taking a right to negative freedom as primary, for example, one might argue that democracy or self-government provides a better guarantee of an adequate realm of life free from interference than any other form of government (Berlin, 1958, 90). Or, taking a right to positive freedom as primary, one may argue that a substantial area free from interference is a necessary condition for meaningful self-government, i.e., the freedom to determine for oneself what one will be and do. Still, which of these conceptions one takes as more fundamental can have important implications for the weight one attaches to various rights, as well as for other components of one's moral and political views.

It is perhaps worth noting that the right to make or participate meaningfully in decisions importantly affecting one's life, the more general right of self-determination, and the ideal of autonomy, all of which found their way into more or less central roles in the discussions earlier in this book, involve positive, not negative liberty. On the other hand, libertarian philosopher Robert Nozick, who questions whether there is any right to a say in those decisions which importantly affect one, seems to conceive of rights exclusively in terms of negative liberties within a realm defined by the limits of one's property (Nozick, 1974; see my Chapter Two note 19 for relevant quotes and discussion).

A somewhat different distinction sometimes drawn between negative and positive freedom takes negative freedom as including, in addition to the absence of interference, some of Berlin's positive liberties, such as participation in the political process. But one's ability actually to enjoy or exercise these liberties may depend on access to material resources one does not have.[4] A positive interpretation of these freedoms would include access to the necessary conditions for their exercise.

Berlin, as I understand him, would reject this formulation, although he is sympathetic to the point that those who use it want to make. In Berlin's view, however, if someone is not in a position to exercise his or her freedom because he or she is hungry, illiterate, or wracked by disease, what that person needs is food, education, or medical care, not a different kind of freedom. Up to some level, these other needs are more urgent than freedom, but there is no reason to confuse them with freedom (Berlin, 1958, 86–7). On the other hand, if one believes that poverty is the cause of the hunger, illiteracy, or disease, and that the poverty is caused (intentionally or not) by the actions and arrangements of others, then lack of freedom *is* involved, but it is lack of freedom in Berlin's negative sense of non-interference (Berlin, 1958, 85). That is, the poor people's freedom to act to meet their own nutritional and medical needs is interfered with (intentionally or not) by the actions of others. If this sort of indirect and often unintentional interference is taken seriously, the idea of negative freedom could turn out to be much more substantive than many of its adherents would like.

Berlin's point seems well taken with regard to terming the contrast between freedom and the ability to do what one is free to do as a matter of negative versus positive *freedom*. It does seem appropriate, however, to speak of a contrast between negative and positive—or perhaps better, formal and substantive—*rights*. As Bernard Williams says of the right to equality before the law:

> It may be said that in a certain society, men have equal rights to a fair trial, to seek redress from the law for wrongs committed agains them, etc. But if a fair trial or redress from the law can be secured in that society only by moneyed and educated persons, to insist that everyone *has* this right, though only these particular persons can *secure* it, rings hollow to the point of cynicism: we are concerned not with the abstract existence of rights, but with the extent to which those rights govern what actually happens. [Williams, 1962, 128–29]

The right to equality of opportunity for women and minority group members, in the absence of positive affirmative action measures, has the same hollow ring.

The idea of non-interference central to Berlin's negative freedom also plays a role in the contrast between formal and substantive rights. Understood formally, the right to equal treatment before the law is thought to be satisfied provided that the law itself does not, for example, preclude the poor from retaining counsel—it is only their poverty that may prevent them. Equality of opportunity, in the most purely formal sense, is achieved if no one is ruled ineligible in advance to compete for jobs, admission to professional or apprentice-ship programs, etc. Purely formal rights, then, are deemed satisfied so long as there is no explicit governmental or other direct interference with persons attempting to exercise them. This point is clearly illustrated by an example from our earlier discussion where we may observe movement toward a purely formal interpretation of constitutional rights on the part of the Supreme Court. Upholding the constitutionality of restrictions on the funding of abortions, the Court held that although government may not place obstacles in the way of a person's exercise of a constitutionally protected right, it need not remove obstacles not of its own creation.

Another contemporary dispute is over the relative weight of what are termed personal and political rights on the one hand and economic, social, and cultural rights on the other. The former involve bodily integrity and security (the right not to be arbitrarily seized and tortured, for example), civil liberties, and rights of democratic participation, such as the right to vote. These rights are widely taken to be more stringent than the economic, social, and cultural rights which include the right to minimally adequate food, shelter, and health care to sustain life. U. S. foreign policy, for example, while it may be justly criticized for honoring even the former in word but not in deed, does not honor the latter even in word. Critics argue that this way of categorizing and prioritizing rights is unjustifiable—that some economic rights belong among the rights with highest priority, along with some rights of bodily security and integrity. This argument is perhaps most fully and convincingly made by Henry Shue. Once again, the negative-positive rights theme emerges in a somewhat different form:

> Frequently it is asserted or assumed that a highly significant difference between rights to physical security and rights to subsistence is that they are respectively "negative" rights and "positive" rights.

> Now the basic idea behind the general suggestion that there are positive rights and negative rights seems to have been that one kind of rights (the positive ones) require other people to act positively—to "do something"—whereas another kind of rights (the negative ones) require other people merely to refrain from acting in certain ways—to do nothing that violates the rights. For example, according to this picture, a right to subsistence would be positive because it would require other people, in the last resort, to supply food or clean air to those unable to find, produce, or buy their own; a right to security would be negative because it would require other people merely to refrain from murdering or otherwise assaulting those with the right. [Shue, 1980, 35–37]

The supposed priority of the negative over the positive rights, then, is thought to derive from the fact that the former make less stringent demands on others in terms of correlative duties, while the demands made by the latter are potentially so great as to be ruinous. Notice that the negative rights are again associated with non-interference; we are thought to satisfy them by leaving people alone. Shue argues that the distinction is vastly overdrawn. He points out that the right to physical security engenders not merely the demand that others leave the person alone but also that they arrange to protect that person from others, whether among themselves or from outside, who pose threats to his or her security. Thus the positive demands of the right to physical security are substantial, and are in fact far from satisfied in some cities of our own nation. To the objection that he has blurred an important distinction between rights to physical security (which require that others not assault one) and rights to protection from assault (which require more positive steps), Shue replies: "Insofar as this frail distinction holds up, it is the rights-to-be-protected-against-assaults that any reasonable person would demand from society. A demand for physical security is not normally a demand simply to be left alone, but a demand to be protected against harm" (Shue, 1980, 38–39). To assert that the right to physical security can be satisfied by leaving people alone is to give it a purely formal interpretation. Shue goes on to point out that the right to subsistence can often be satisfied by protecting the right holder from actions of others that would destroy his or her capacity to meet his or her own subsistence needs. He concludes:

> Making the necessary provisions for the fulfillment of subsistence rights may sometimes be burdensome, especially when the task is to recover from past neglect of basic duties. But we have no reason to believe, as proponents of the negative/positive distinction typically assert, that the performance of the duties correlative to subsistence rights would always or usually be more difficult, more expensive, less praticable, or harder to "deliver" than would the actual performance of the duties correlative to the rights that are conventionally labeled negative and that are more often announced than in fact fulfilled. [Shue, 1980, 63]

Shue argues that, if any positive-negative distinction between rights can be maintained at all, it cannot be used to justify giving priority to negative over positive rights.

There is, then, something of a pattern to these disputes, so that someone who favors Berlin's negative conception of liberty is perhaps more likely to be satisfied with a formal than with a substantive interpretation of rights and is apt to give priority to security rights over subsistence rights. It is no doubt clear that I would favor the other side—the more positive and substantive conceptions—in each instance. Indeed, the case for the more substantive, positive conceptions becomes compelling as the inadequacies of the formal, negative conceptions become evident. As it becomes clear, for example, that the formal rights to vote, to due process, and equal protection do little or nothing to establish political equality or equal treatment before the law, the case is made for the claim that justice, as it is conceived in our society, requires more than purely formal rights. The main point I want to bring out here is that these theoretical disputes express very practical differences over the direction our way of life should take.

Rights are not fixed, but arise out of relatively (though not entirely) fixed basic human needs in combination with continuously changing historical circumstances. The needs, which can only be characterized in the most general terms in abstraction from historical circumstances, take different forms and thus give rise to different specific rights depending on material conditions (e.g., the level and kind of technology, availability of resources, etc.), social relations, and the beliefs and state of knowledge prevalent at a particular time and place. I do not mean to claim that the historical circumstances involved in the determination of rights typically change quickly or suddenly or often, but change they do. As a result, some rights change their shape; some lapse because no longer applicable; new rights arise, sometimes in conflict with old rights which must adjust or give way. And it is conceivable that conditions could change sufficiently so that rights might disappear entirely. (I shall come back to this idea below.)

One need not believe that rights are universal or eternal to believe that, in a world in which they exist, they are extremely important. They exist in our world (and at this point in history our world includes this entire planet). They are important partly because they are, in this world, perhaps the most fundamental aspect of membership in the moral community—and hence a basic expression of respect for moral personhood and a ground of self-respect. It is a central aspect of our nature that we have rights, and we express our nature as moral agents by respecting the rights of others and demanding that our own rights be respected. Given the view that social relations have a large role in constituting the natures of the individuals engaged in them, we can say this without implying that rights are inborn or universal.

Rights have this central role in our conceptions of ourselves and each other largely because they are needed in very concrete ways for survival and effective functioning in practical day-to-day life. To be able to make a living, to make contracts with a reasonable expectation that they will be fulfilled (and to have some recourse if they are not), not to be attacked, robbed, beaten, arbitrarily seized, searched, interrogated, tortured, etc.—these are conditions we need in order to live in dignity to be sure, but they are also conditions we need in order to live and function in tolerable health and security as participants in our world. For ours is a competitive, individualistic world in which rights are often one's only protection against literally or figuratively being knocked down, crushed, trampled by others in their pursuit of their own ends. Rights are, at a minimum, controls or restrictions on what one person or agent may do to others in pursuit of the former's goals. These goals need not be selfish ones, although they often are. I may not—except in special circumstances—violate your rights to promote the interests of a third party any more than I may do so to promote my own interests. Rights also limit—though not absolutely—what government or private parties may do to promote the public good. A person who is without rights, or not in a position to claim or defend his or her rights is quite defenseless in such a world. And if others are in a position to take advantage of his or her condition, life can (and does) become "nasty, brutish, and short." Hobbes's state of nature is the competitive, individualist world with no enforceable rights, i.e., no controls on anyone's pursuit of his or her own ends at the expense of others. As Ronald Dworkin says, "The concept of rights . . . has its most natural use when a political society is divided, and appeals to cooperation or a common goal are pointless" (R. Dworkin, 1978, 184).

The tendency of the rights-oriented perspective to reflect and reinforce the competitive, self-interested character of our world is illustrated by the fact, mentioned in Chapter Four, that U. S. labor law, in establishing the right of workers to engage in concerted activity (collective bargaining, picketing, striking) for mutual benefit, limits the protected activity to the agents' self-interest, narrowly defined. Not protected are acts of working-class solidarity, such as refusing to cross a picket line. And, indeed, some such acts, for example, sympathy strikes and secondary boycotts, are prohibited.

A world without rights need not necessarily be a world without self-respect, as Joel Feinberg, in "The Nature and Value of Rights," claims it must (Feinberg, 1970). Because of the competitive, individualistic, self-protective character of rights, it is conceivable that a genuine community in which the promotion of the good of each were actually the goal of all might have no need for rights as we know them, yet might be equally or more conducive to self-respect than our society is.

In his article, Feinberg asks us to imagine a fictitious society, "Nowheresville—a world very much like our own except that no one, or hardly anyone . . . has *rights*" (Feinberg, 1970, 78).[5] He then argues quite persuasively that something very important, and closely bound up with human dignity and self-respect, is missing from Nowheresville.

But if it is true that, although rights may not have a role in every society—or in every good society—they are extremely important in a society such as ours, then the more like our world Nowheresville is, the more we will feel, correctly, that something very important is missing in Nowheresville. Feinberg does permit us to imagine that benevolence and altruism are more prevalent and more effective in Nowheresville than in our world, and this might be thought to show that, even in a genuine community of the sort I alluded to above, the absence of rights would be a serious moral lack. But Feinberg's Nowheresville includes servants serving benevolent but class-conscious masters, students and contestants competing for grades, prizes, and rewards from masters, teachers, and judges. We must suppose, since Nowheresville is as much as possible like our own society, that the results of these competitions play the same kind of crucial roles in people's lives there as they do here. Yet, although its masters, teachers, and judges generally try to award servants, students, and contestants the rewards, grades and prizes they deserve, "One should be happy that they *ever* treat us well, and not grumble over their occasional lapses. Their hoped for responses, after all are *gratuities*, and there is no wrong in the omission of what is merely gratuitous. Such is the response of persons who have no concept of *rights*, even persons who are proud of their own deserts" (Feinberg, 1970, 82). One needs to imagine a world, not as much as possible like, but as much as possible unlike ours in these and related respects if we are to imagine a morally tolerable world without rights.

As Ruth Anna Putnam says, to suppose that the competitive, individualistic conception of persons on which our concept of rights depends is true independently of social circumstances "suggests that human beings, regardless of changes in the material conditions of life, will always face each other as competitors, will never be in a position to replace what is at best civilized enmity by love, trust or friendship" (Putnam, 1976, 104). Similarly, in an important new book, *Liberalism and the Limits of Justice*, Michael Sandel asks us to imagine a situation in which rights play little or no role, "not because injustice is rampant but because their appeal is preempted by a spirit of generosity in which I am rarely inclined to claim my fair share. Nor does this generosity necessarily imply that I receive out of kindness a share that is equal to or greater than the share I would be entitled to under fair principles of justice. I may get less. The point is not that I get what I would otherwise get, only more spontaneously, but simply that the questions of what I get and what I am due do not loom large in the overall context of this way of life" (Sandel, 1982, 33).

Also, as Allen Buchanan notes, "some of Marx's most trenchant criticisms of alienation in capitalism focus on the ways in which social interaction in capitalism fails to recognize, or even subverts, the distinction between persons and mere things" (Buchanan, 1982, 78). Insofar as proper theoretical and practical recognition of this distinction is central to the idea of respect for persons—as it is, for example, in Kant's injunction that persons always be treated as ends in themselves, and not as mere means—persons in a communitarian society which had no use for the concept of rights might manifest greater respect for self and others than in a rights-oriented society like ours.

Thus we can, and must, acknowledge the crucial importance of rights in a world like ours without supposing that they must have this role in *any* morally acceptable world, and without taking them to be the whole or even a necessary part of the highest moral achievement humans are capable of. On the other hand, should the more substantive, positive view of rights become predominant and continue to develop, it is conceivable that rights might still exist in a genuine community. That is, the language of rights might persist, but their nature and significance would be quite different from what they now are and—even more—from what they historically have been.

Rights, in our world, are important as tools or handles for people to grasp in pressing their needs as these take shape and manifest themselves in the face of existing and changing circumstances. This is partly because the language of rights is the language most people speak in these contexts. There are reasons for that, too. One of the places people must fight out conflicts in our society is the courts. As we saw in Chapter Four, the rights to organize, bargain collectively, and strike had—and still have—to be fought for in the courts and legislatures as well as on the streets and picket lines, because employers would—and still do—get injunctions, charge people with conspiracy, and have them put in jail. Even to get your case heard in court it is necessary to define it in terms the courts find relevant, and this generally means in terms of rights.[6] Since the courts are the primary upholders of legal rights, and rights are the primary legal tools or weapons of self-defense, the rights-oriented perspective is very influential in the way people perceive and define their situations. And this is practical because to a large degree, at least in the short run, this perspective dictates the terms within which we must fight our day-to-day battles, whether in the courts, on the streets, in the media, or—most likely—some combination of these. As David Lyons says, "Rights are the principal currency of moral, political, and legal disputes" (Lyons, 1979, 1).

Rights can, of course, be controversial, as the disputes discussed above clearly show. But once the courts or the legislature declare that persons have certain rights, then political and legal arguments have to proceed according to different rules. The burden of proof, so to speak, shifts, and the opposition has to show that the consequences of respecting such rights in specific circumstances will be, not just worse than not respecting them, but so terrible as to justify the suppression or restriction of rights. Similarly, if a policy gets put into effect on grounds of rights, it is not quite as vulnerable as one based solely on the general good. It will be more difficult a few years later, successfully to attack such a policy on the grounds that it did not turn out to have the expected consequences. Thus, if one can get one's position hooked securely to a right, one has something relatively firm to hang on to—*if* one is in a position effectively to claim one's rights.

Rights are important also, insofar as they are legally recognized and enforced, in that they provide the space, so to speak, within which action on other matters can take place. Rights to free speech allow individuals to criticize authorities and laws, call problems to the attention of others, propose changes, and so on. The rights to picket and leaflet allow workers to publicize and explain their position to other workers and to the public. The right to strike allows them to bring concerted economic pressure on the employer in an effort to improve their situation. Without legal recognition of these rights, such activities would still go on, as they did before the rights were legally established, but they would be severely hampered.

Rights played a progressive role in breaking down the powers and prerogatives of the feudal aristocracy. And the strong tendency of the rights perspective to see rights as applying not in virtue of station, wealth, position, etc., but in spite of them, and in virtue solely of one's being a person, has lent itself to further progressive developments. Arguments for the more substantive, positive interpretation of rights rely heavily on this aspect, claiming that if rights are something everyone is entitled to just by virtue of being human (or, less ahistorically, of being a member of a particular kind of moral community) then one's capacity to exercise one's rights should not be contingent upon wealth, power or position. The civil rights and women's movements pressed the point with regard to race, national origin, sex, etc. Earlier, rights to political participation, originally restricted to property owners, were extended to all male citizens on the same grounds. As rights have evolved, the connection between acknowledging a person's rights and respecting him or her as a person, and hence, in some sense, as an equal, has been a dynamic force in movements for expansion of old rights and recognition of new ones.

On the other hand, there are some ways in which appeal to rights may circumscribe our thinking and have a conservative influence. Often when complex social issues are cast in terms of competing or conflicting rights, the question becomes simply which right outweighs the other. This can distort the issue and deflect attention from other relevant factors and important questions. When the issue of abortion is framed as a conflict between the rights of the pregnant woman and the rights of the fetus, for example, a wide range of important and relevant social factors are ignored. Consider also issues such as the right of, say, teachers or hospital workers to strike. It is very convenient for administrators, school and hospital boards, etc. to present it as a conflict between the right of the teachers to strike versus the right of students to an education, or the right of hospital workers to strike versus the right of patients to receive care. This deflects attention, first, from the issues involved in such a strike (in which the interests of teachers and students, hospital workers and patients often coincide) and, second, from the background conditions for this supposed conflict of rights, which are, in effect, accepted as given. We are asked simply to weigh the rights on both sides and decide which should prevail, not to consider whether and why such a conflict should arise in the first place—what are the social arrangements that place two groups in intolerable circumstances and set things up so that they (apparently) have to fight each other for any improvements? It is often the case that in such situations both groups, whose rights are presented as conflicting, are relatively powerless and actually have many interests in common, including an interest in promoting social arrangements in which conflicts of this sort would not arise.

Consider, for example, the presentation of issues concerning affirmative action as conflicts between the rights of female and minority workers on one hand and white male workers on the other. Or posing issues of immigration policy in terms of the rights of actual or potential immigrant workers versus the rights of U. S. citizen workers. We are encouraged, by this way of formulating the issues, to accept as given the social and economic institutions that place people in competition for the opportunity to make a living. In many cases there really is no possible acceptable resolution of such issues within the existing background conditions.

Thus, more powerful persons or groups who benefit from the existing arrangements can not only avoid having those arrangements challenged, but they benefit further from suppression of one group's rights in the name of the other group while themselves appearing to stand above the fray as uninvolved objective observers, weighing the merits on both sides, chastising one group or the other (and frequently both) for making unreasonable demands or adopting unreasonable tactics.

Another way in which the rights-oriented perspective is limited emerges from our discussion of the possibility that there could be a morally acceptable, even good, society without rights: the minimalist, individualistic, and egoistic character of rights. Examining the rights of liberty, property, equality, and security proclaimed by the French Declaration of the Rights of Man and by the U. S. Constitution, Karl Marx observed:

> Liberty is . . . the right to do everything which does not harm others. . . . It is a question of the liberty of man regarded as an isolated monad, withdrawn into himself. . . . Liberty as a right of man is not founded upon the relations between man and man, but rather upon the separation of man from man. It is the right of such separation. The right of the *circumscribed* individual, withdrawn into himself.
>
> The right of property is . . . the right to enjoy one's fortune and dispose of it as one will; without regard for other men and independently of society. . . . It is the right of self-interest. . . . It leads every man to see in other men, not the *realization*, but rather the *limitation* of his own liberty.
>
> The term "equality" has here no political significance. It is only the equal right to liberty as defined above; namely that every man is equally regarded as a self-sufficient monad.
>
> Security is the supreme social concept of civil society . . . The whole society exists only in order to guarantee for each of its members the preservation of his person, his rights and his property. [Marx, 1843, 42–43. Emphasis in original.]

He sums up:

> The only bond between men is natural necessity, need and private interest, the preservation of their property and their egoistic persons. [Marx, 1843, 43]

Later, in his "Critique of the Gotha Program," Marx discusses a much more substantive conception of the notion of equal rights than that described above. According to this conception, differences in inheritance, wealth, power, etc. would not only be barred from influencing one's treatment before the law (the right to vote, to due process, etc.). Such differences would no longer influence how a person fared in society as a whole. The only effective way to achieve this is substantially to eliminate such differences from society. Each individual would be entitled to consumption goods on an equal basis: the amount one is entitled to would be determined by the amount of work time one has contributed.

> Content and form are changed, because under the altered circumstances no one can give anything except his labour, and because, on the other hand, nothing can pass to the ownership of individuals except individual means of consumption. But as far as the distribution of the latter among the individual producers is concerned, the same principle prevails as in the exchange of commodity-equivalents. [Marx, 1875, 530]

He goes on to criticize this new conception:

> In spite of this advance, this *equal right* is still constantly stigmatized by a bourgeois limitation. The right of the producers is *proportional* to the labour they supply; the equality consists in the fact that measurement is made by an *equal standard*, labour.
> But one man is superior to another physically or mentally and so supplies more labour in the same time, or can labour for longer time; and labour, to serve as a measure, must be defined by its duration or intensity, otherwise it ceases to be a standard of measurement. This *equal* right is an unequal right for unequal labour. It recognises no class differences, because everyone is only a worker like everyone else; but it tacitly recognises unequal individual endowment and thus productive capacity as natural privileges. *It is therefore, a right of inequality, in its content, like every right.* Right by its very nature can consist only in the application of an equal standard; but unequal individuals are measurable only by an equal standard insofar as they are brought under an equal point of view, are taken from one *definite* side only, for instance, in the present case, are regarded *only as workers* and nothing more is seen in them, everything else being ignored. Further, one worker is married, another not; one has more children than another, and so on. . . . Thus, with an equal performance of labour, and hence an equal share in the social consumption fund, one will in fact receive more than another, one will be richer than another, and so on. [Marx, 1875, 530–31. Emphasis in original.]

Marx goes on to say that only after our way of life had changed in many other fundamental ways—only when, in Sandel's words, "the questions of what I get and what I am due do not loom large in the overall context of this way of life" (Sandel, 1982, 33)—would it be possible to transcend these limitations. Hence, recognition of these limitations in no way diminishes the importance of rights in our world. Indeed, moving toward more substantive, positive interpretations of rights appears to be a way of moving in the direction of more genuine community.

A point closely related to that concerning the individualistic, competitive character of rights is that they are not just minimalist, but remedial, as is the concept of justice with which they are associated. David Hume wrote:

> [J]ustice takes its rise from human conventions; and . . . these are intended as a remedy to some inconveniences, which proceed from the concurrence of certain *qualities* of the human mind with the *situation* of external objects. The qualities of the mind are *selfishness* and *limited generosity*: And the situation of external objects is their *easy change*, join'd to their *scarcity* in comparison of the wants and desires of men. . . . Encrease to a sufficient degree the benevolence of men, or the bounty of nature, and you render justice useless, by supplying its place with much nobler virtues, and more valuable blessings. [Hume, 1739, 494–95. Emphasis in original.]

Sandel puts the point succinctly: "Justice is the first virtue of social institutions not absolutely, as truth is to theories, but only conditionally, as physical courage is to a war zone" (Sandel, 1982, 31).

It must be acknowledged that acceptance of my view of rights, although it emphasizes the importance of rights in our world, may nevertheless weaken the force of rights-based claims as compared to views of rights as absolute, inherent, inviolable, universal, eternal, or whatnot. Recognizing that rights may change, come into or go out of existence, be overridden or defeated, depending on historical or other circumstances may appear to take away whatever bite rights are supposed to have. The prospects of establishing once and for all, in any practical conflict involving purported rights, which ones are real and which not, or which take precedence if both are real, seem much dimmer if rights cannot be counted on to remain fixed over time while we ponder what they are and how they measure up against each other.

But this is not to say that it is just a matter of opinion which purported rights are real and which rights take precedence. Rights are based on needs, and though needs take various shapes and forms, and are of various kinds, some are more fundamental than others, and differing historical circumstances will determine various necessary conditions for the satisfaction of fundamental needs, and various relations among needs. A correct assessment of all of these factors will determine, in particular historical conditions, what rights if any there are and what their relative weights are.[7]

This is not to say that there are not situations in which conflicts of rights cannot justly be settled within the existing background conditions. Indeed, such situations are common, as we saw above. In such situations, insistence on the importance of upholding both sets of rights, even if it means basic changes in social arrangements, can be a significant force for social change. In this way, the promises, needs, and expectations to which a system of beliefs and institutional arrangements gives rise can generate, from within, a fundamental critique of that same system.

Here, then, is my response to the argument that it is counterproductive to state one's objections to the wrongs people suffer in our society in terms of rights or justice, since this may suggest, falsely, that the system could be rendered morally acceptable by a few reforms. If the only game in town is one whose rules are stacked against you, and you have no choice but to play, you have a valid complaint. If, in addition, some of the other players cheat, even according to the lopsided rules, you have another valid complaint. And it is worth doing something about the latter even if—*especially* if—you cannot, in the short run, do much about the former. The problem, then, is how to keep one's eye on the ball, so to speak—how not to lose sight, in theory or in practice, of the former complaint, in one's efforts to address the never-ending series of complaints of the latter sort. Part of the answer, I think, is as follows. If the truth is that cheating cannot be eliminated, that the rules of the game cannot all be satisfied in practice—either because the rules are mutually inconsistent or because they presuppose factual claims that are false, or both—then, as attempts to eliminate cheating inevitably, at least partially, fail, the deeper flaws in the game are progressively exposed. Thus complaints of the second kind are what give rise to complaints of the first kind. Call complaints of the second kind *internal* critiques and complaints of the first kind *external* critiques.[8] An internal critique, then, criticizes the workings of a system from within, so to speak, in that system's own terms. An external critique criticizes the system as a whole, and thus takes up a perspective outside the system. I am suggesting that internal critiques, by exposing the limits of the degree to which a system is capable of responding to them, can give rise to more fundamental, or external critiques of that system. (In addition, for an external critique, one needs to have some conception of an alternative system.)

Internal criticisms are important in their own right. Persons are seriously wronged when their important rights are violated, and the fact that one cannot eliminate all wrongs is no reason not to notice and attempt to do something about those one can address. They are important also in that they play a necessary dialectical role in the generation of external criticisms. This is so especially when important connections among the various internal criticisms are perceived. One of the aims of this book has been to explore some of those connections.

Current social arrangements grant in theory and in form, though not in substance, what both slavery and serfdom, each in its own way, denied: the dignity and autonomy of every individual, the right of each to significant control of his or her life and destiny. The demand that the substance be added to the form, that practice fulfill what theory promises, may ultimately press beyond the limits of what these arrangements—even significantly reformed—can deliver.

Notes

Chapter One

1. Since this chapter was written, this controversy has been at least partially resolved by the Supreme Court in the Cotton Dust case (*American Textile Manufacturer's Institute* v. *Donovan* 452 U.S. [1981]). In 1981, the Court found that, in the OSH Act, "Congress itself defined the basic relationships between costs and benefits, by placing the 'benefit' of worker health above all other considerations save those making attainment of this benefit unachievable." Thus, cost-benefit studies were deemed inappropriate for the setting of OSHA standards, and "feasibility" was interpreted broadly as consistency with the continued viability of the industry as a whole.

2. See, for example, Nozick, 1969; Pennock and Chapman, 1972; Frankfurt, 1973; Lyons, 1975; Cohen, 1979; Zimmerman, 1981; Fowler, 1982; and Cohen, 1983.

3. See Zimmerman, 1981.

4. Obviously, we have to do here with what might be called "natural necessity," not logical necessity.

5. For other examples, details and discussion, see: Stellman, 1977, 35–39 and 178–200; and Milkman, 1980, entire.

6. Reflection upon this fact is what led me to the somewhat different way of thinking about paternalism to be discussed in Chapter Two.

7. It may at first appear that this identification of the interests of the parent with those of the child makes nonsense of the primary meaning of the term "paternalism." But this may instead be the reason why paternalism in the parent-child relationship is (or has been until quite recently) generally considered unproblematic. Parents are counted on to treat their children's interests as their own, to love their children as themselves. Thus, it is only paternalism outside of this special relationship that is thought to stand in need of explicit justification. That this picture of the parent-child relationship is idealized and often, if not always, false does not prevent it from influencing our thinking on the subject. Also, this way of thinking may constitute a link between contemporary individualism and an earlier, explicitly patriarchal world in which one person, the paterfamilias, defines and represents the interest of the entire family.

8. Milkman cites Alice Kessler-Harris, " 'Where are the Organized Women Workers?'," *Feminist Studies*, Vol. 3, No. 1/2 (Fall 1975): 92–110. Kessler-Harris cites the *American Federationist* 7 (April 1900). (Additional examples may be found in Stellman, 1977, 35–39 and 176.)

9. Women's Occupational Health Resources Center *News*, Nov/Dec. 1979, 6.

10. The reasoning in two Supreme Court decisions upholding the constitutionality of restrictions on the funding of abortions for poor women (*Maher* v. *Roe*, 1977, and *Harris* v. *McRae*, 1980) is a potentially devastating rejection of this way of thinking. The Court held that although government may not place obstacles in the way of a person's exercise of a constitutionally protected rights, it need not remove obstacles not of its own creation.

11. Keeping in mind that reproductive hazards can affect men as well as women, note that widespread acceptance of the practice of employing only infertile workers in these jobs would lead to the creation of a subclass of "drones" in our society. A person who genuinely chooses to have him- or herself sterilized because having children does not fit into his or her life-plan is not at issue; a class of workers required to be sterilized in order to get and hold their jobs is.

Chapter Two

1. DBCP is one of these; yet a California county agricultural commissioner suggested that field workers "protect" themselves in this way so that the state's ban on DBCP use might be lifted (Ben-Horin, 1979, 62).

2. The Agent Orange ingredient containing dioxin is the herbicide 2,4,5-T which was banned for most domestic uses March 1, 1979 by the EPA following a study linking the spray—diluted far below Vietnam levels—to increased miscarriages in women in rural Oregon (*Daily Record*, Northwest New Jersey, April 1, 1979). 2,4,5-T is still used on rice and soybean crops as well as grazing lands for cattle; a complete ban is under consideration (*In These Times*, April 2–8, 1980).

3. Many public employees are denied some of the rights and protections of other workers. For example, federal agencies are not subject to OSHA regulations and enforcement provisions, though they are expected to have health and safety programs that are consistent with OSHA standards and to report to OSHA annually on their health and safety efforts. State and local governments are not subject to OSHA at all in their role as employers; no public employees at any level are covered by the National Labor Relations Act. (Postal workers, since 1974, are considered quasi-private employees and hence are covered.)

4. But we should not ignore the question as related to adult farm workers and "volunteer" servicemen and women. For these groups of workers typically have the fewest available alternatives. Hence the "consent" they give in accepting a job is questionable. Moreover, they often are not adequately informed of the risks they face.

5. Of course, now that they do know (although DBCP production has been discontinued, they are aware that this and other risks may be present in other chemicals they work with) the question of genuine consent given restricted options arises for them too. Recall Jack Hodge's "Where else are you going to go?" and the other worker who is consciously trading his own life expectancy for the wherewithal to raise his family.

6. I owe this example to Tim Scanlon, to whom I am also grateful for discussion of many points along the way.

7. It is curious, but irrelevant, that "sterile" and "sterilization" are not related grammatically in the same way as "fertile" and "fertilization"; the grammatical parallel of "sterile" is "fertilized."

8. Whatever one thinks of this distinction, though, it is a gross distortion to suggest, as the head of the National Peach Council did in an incredible letter to then-OSHA Director, Eula Bingham, that people might volunteer to work with DBCP as a means of getting around religious bans on birth control (Ben-Horin, 1979, 63).

9. If a person were sterilized as a result of an illness or accident for which no other person was responsible in any way, it would perhaps not strictly be false, but it would certainly be strange and misleading to say that he or she had been sterilized without informed consent.

10. It also seems plausible to suppose that duration of exposure is a factor leading first to reduced sperm count and eventually to sterilization. So the numbers would have to be relativized to duration, in which case the risk of sterility might approach or reach 1 with long enough exposure. So (c) would include (a) as one extreme.

11. Information in the last three paragraphs is from (Spencer, 1977, 184–92) and (Berman, 1978, 41–44). These are among the reasons why health and safety advocates are alarmed at proposals that employers in hazardous industries be exempt from general OSHA inspections if employer injury and illness logs or state workers' compensation records show lower-than-industry-average injury and illness rates.

12. For example, what is the nature of that relationship? Is it an ordinary contractual one? If so, what are the explicit and implicit terms of the contract (and should the presumed implicit terms be made explicit)? What, if any, are the special rights and duties involved in this relationship? What is the basis of the patient's right to privacy, and what are its limits? May the physician do whatever is necessary to promote the

health of the patient, even if this means using resources without which others will be far worse off than the patient would be without them? Can the physician have conflicting duties to different patients, and how should they be resolved? Does the physician have the right, or even the duty, to withhold certain information from a patient, and if so why and under what circumstances?

13. Once we begin to think about doctors as employees, the following questions arise: What are the differences and similarities between the issues facing company doctors and those facing doctors employed, wholly or partly, by hospitals or other medical institutions? To what extent are physicians in private practice in effect becoming employees of insurance companies, as increasing proportions of their payments come directly from those sources and only indirectly from their patients? How does each of these different situations affect the actual doctor-patient relationship, and how does this compare with the way we tend to think of it (independent self-employed professional and individual client in a one-to-one contractual relationship arrived at in a free market)? And how do these various situations bear on issues such as the right of doctors and other medical employees to strike?

14. A compromise position, that has been proposed (but which I would oppose) would be to permit, in certain cases where trade-secret status is established, withholding the generic name of a substance, but require labeling and posting of the symptoms of chronic and acute exposure, emergency procedures, and the like. One reason I would be opposed to such a compromise is that workers and their representatives might want to have independent studies done of the effects of the substance, or conduct independent monitoring of exposure levels, or research the scientific literature on the substance. It seems to me that they have a right to do these things—a right that is stronger than trade secret rights.

15. For arguments against physicians withholding or falsifying information, see for example, Buchanan, 1978, and Goldman, 1980, chapter Four. For arguments in favor of withholding information when authorized to do so, see VanDeVeer, 1980.

16. To what extent is the education our system provides for future workers geared to preparing them to participate in an active, informed way in decisions that importantly affect their lives, and to what extent does it prepare them passively to accept discipline and defer to experts? (Bowles and Gintis, 1976, argue that it is geared overwhelmingly to the latter.) If people generally have a right to self-determination, then it is at least arguable that they have a right to an education geared to preparing them for self-determination. It is not just arguable, but compelling, that they have a right not to be subjected to an "education" geared to undermining self-determination. And if that is the education necessary to prepare people for the world of work as it exists today, then if people have a right to self-determination, the world of work as it exists today is incompatible with that right—and what people need is an education that prepares them to change it.

17. There is currently a controversy at a large northeastern state university over health hazards in a building which houses animal laboratories, academic offices and classrooms. I am told that two professors, both with Ph.D.s, who expressed concern about working in the building were privately described as "hysterical" by university officials, who refused to permit teachers temporarily to move their classes to other available classrooms because they were afraid of "creating a panic." Apparently, no amount of education is sufficient to enable workers to respond rationally when they believe their health is in danger.

18. In a conference presentation (Sass, 1977), Robert Sass, Director of the Occupational Health and Safety Division, Saskatchewan Department of Labour, cites a study (Meissner, 1971) which shows that the nature of work is the single most important factor in determining one's leisure pattern. He cites another study (Cronin, 1971) that indicates that worker rights pertaining to working conditions correlated positively (as none of the traditional causes of accidents did) with reduction of accidents. Other factors, such as night shift work or rotating shifts have obvious and profound effects on family and social life. For further discussions and illustrations of the influence of work

on all aspects of life, including self-esteem, see Braverman, 1974; Sennett and Cobb, 1973; and Terkel, 1974.

19. There are *some* decisions which may importantly affect an individual's life, yet which that person has no right to make or even to participate in, for example, decisions which some other person or group has the right to make. X and Y both participate in the decision that they shall become lovers. But suppose that X wants to become lovers with Y, while Y does not reciprocate. Y's negative decision may importantly affect X's life; still, it is Y's decision to make. Presumably this is because Y's right of self-determination requires that Y have veto power in matters of this sort. Neither party has the right to make the positive decision alone since each has the right to make a negative decision—neither has the right to decide they *shall* become lovers since each has the right to decide they shall *not*. An adequate account of the right of self-determination would have to say much more about what kinds of decisions it does and does not apply to, and why.

According to Robert Nozick, "After we exclude from consideration the decisions which others have a right to make, and the actions which would aggress against me, steal from me, and so on, and hence violate *my* (Lockean) rights, it is not clear that there are *any* decisions remaining about which even to raise the question of whether I have a right to a say in those that importantly affect me" (Nozick, 1974, 270, his emphasis). This is because his view of rights is entirely property-oriented, and he regards property rights as very nearly absolute and inviolable. He says, for example, "Other people's rights and entitlements to *particular things (that* pencil, *their* body, and so on) and how they choose to exercise these rights and entitlements fix the external environment of any given individual and the means that will be available to him. . . . There are particular rights over particular things held by particular persons. . . . No rights exist in conflict with this substructure of particular rights. . . . The particular rights over things fill the space of rights. . . ." (Nozick, 1974, 238, his emphasis). My view, in contrast, is that property rights are not basic, but derive from a combination of other rights, such as subsistence, personal security, privacy and self-determination. A person's rights over his or her body are not *property* rights as Nozick's parenthetical examples say they are. One's body is not a *thing*, on a par with a pencil. It isn't that no one else can own you because you own yourself. We aren't the kinds of entities that ought to be owned at all. In my view, therefore, property rights must often give way in the face of conflicting rights of subsistence, security, privacy, or self-determination.

Chapter Three

1. In either case (a) or (b), if the employer's version is accepted, the worker is precluded from collecting unemployment insurance in many states. One cannot collect in most states if one quits voluntarily or is fired "for cause."

2. It is neither necessary nor sufficient that a legal safety standard be violated before a worker may be justified in refusing an unsafe assignment. A violation may not be serious and may pose no immediate danger, hence, the assignment is not unsafe in the requisite sense. So violation is not sufficient for justified refusal. On the other hand, there may be no specific standard covering a particular hazard which nevertheless poses a serious and immediate threat. In such a case, I claim, refusal is justified; so violation is not a necessary condition for justified refusal. So far, I am not talking about the *legal* status of the right to refuse; we shall come to that later.

3. Even if there is no written contract, or no explicit mention of health and safety in an existing contract, presumably fulfilling one's legal obligations as an employer may be understood as implicit in any employment agreement.

4. Unless the union agrees in the contract to give it up, workers do have the right to strike over contract violations. But we are talking now about an individual or several individuals refusing a particular assignment, not about a strike.

5. Insubordination is generally accepted as, and is explicitly recognized in many

union contracts as grounds for dismissal. (In most contracts, management has the right to fire for just cause, and in many 'just cause' is spelled out as including insubordination.) This reflects the traditional view that strict plant discipline is an important employer prerogative. It is revealing that failure to be subordinate should be grounds for voiding what purports to be a voluntary contract among equals.

6. These committees also have the following rights: to veto any plans for new machines, materials, or work processes for health and safety reasons; to decide how to spend the company health and safety budget; to approve the selection and direct the work of the company doctor, nurse, safety engineer, or industrial hygienist; to review all corporate medical records, monitoring results, and other information on hazards; and to decide how much time they need to do their safety committee work, all of which must be paid for by the company. (Witt and Early, 1980, 22)

7. This is true for large international unions such as the Steelworkers (U.S.W.A.), but many smaller unions have only recently begun to get any safety provisions at all into their contracts. (Even if all union contracts did have such provisions, that would cover only about 20 percent of the U.S. workforce.)

8. Stellman and Daum report on the effects of mercury as follows:

. . . Whenever it is left open to the atmosphere, mercury vapor will be present.

Mercury is stored mainly in the kidneys, but its most striking effects are on the nervous system. A person with mercury poisoning can develop a slight tremor of the hands and no longer be able to write properly. Before that, there may be emotional problems such as anxiety, indecision, embarrassment, and depression, and also excessive blushing and sweating. Mercury poisoning can lead to speech disorders and loss of coordination. The victim may develop a staggering gait. Serious changes in mental ability and personality may occur. The expression 'mad as a hatter' refers to the fact that most hatters used to become crazy after practicing their profession over the years. The mercury they used to soften the felt in the hats poisoned them and eventually drove them mad.

Mercury also affects the vision and the eye reflexes. It particularly affects the mouth and teeth, causing loose teeth and sore gums. The kidneys may also be damaged.

These serious and often irreversible effects make it imperative to prevent all exposure to mercury vapor and other forms of mercury. . . [pp.255-56]

9. In 1980, OSHA had enough inspectors to inspect each workplace once every eighty years; average fines were less than $60 per violation, and standards to control the tens of thousands of toxic substances were being issued at the average rate of fewer than three per year (Witt and Early, 1980, 21). These figures can be expected to drop drastically during the Reagan administration.

10. This account of the case and ruling is compiled from the following sources: *In These Times*, March 12–25, 1980; *Home News*, February 27, 1980; LOHP *Monitor*, Vol. 8, no. 2, March–April, 1980; *Daily World*, February 28, 1980.

11. In West Germany, the Protection Against Dismissals Act, passed in 1969, bars the "socially unjustified" dismissal of any worker after a probationary period of six months. The law is enforced by labor courts whose effectiveness originally was undermined by long administrative delays (up to five and six years in some cases). Now the unions can veto any individual discharge for "cause," and the worker stays on the job until the labor court decides. Cases are settled much more promptly now (*Economic Dislocation*, 23–24).

12. Employers are prohibited from *threatening* to shut down or move in order to discourage unionization or to influence contract negotiations. They are not prohibited from *warning* of or *predicting* a potential shutdown or move. For employees, the prospect is threatening either way.

13. *Steelworkers, Local 1130* v. *U.S. Steel Corp.*, 492 F. Supp. 1, 103 LRMM 2925, 2931 (N.D. Ohio 1980). Quoted in DeCarvalho, *et al.*, 1981, 1–2.

14. Information in this paragraph is from *Economic Dislocation*, Joint Report of Study Tour Participants, 1979, UAW, USWA, IAM.

15. Under section 14(b) of the Taft-Hartley Act, states may enact laws prohibiting the negotiation of union security clauses in union contracts. A union security clause provides that all employees within the bargaining unit must join the union after the probationary period for newly hired workers, usually thirty to ninety days. This makes it much easier for employers to break a union by hiring anti-union employees who, by both example and argument convince others to become "free-riders." Many southern states have such laws, resulting in the lowest percentages of unionized workers in the country and the lowest wages in the country—prompting opponents of these laws to call them "right to work-for-less" laws. (See Chapter Four for further discussion.)

16. These variations are set forth in (DeCarvalho, *et al.*, 1981, § VI).

17. There are, of course, consequentialist considerations in favor of these practices, too, and these may be part of what gives rise to the property right and gives it this particular shape. A worker who has worked at a job for many years is likely to be older and have more difficulty finding another comparable job. One who has worked at a job for several years is likely to be settled and have heavy home and family responsibilities. But if these considerations were directly responsible for the practices mentioned, age and family responsibilities rather than seniority would be the appropriate pegs.

18. The Swedish approach to job loss places highest priority on finding the affected worker another job, rejecting the notion that early retirement, even with full pension, is an adequate substitute for a job. This shows a commitment to the idea that persons have a right to make a productive contribution to society. As a result, unemployment in Sweden is just over 2 percent (*Economic Dislocation*, 10, 12, 15). Even this is too high.

19. As I am using the terms, "self-esteem" and "self-respect," these attitudes toward oneself are distinct but related. To esteem someone is to hold that person in high regard, to have a favorable opinion of him or her. To respect someone is to acknowledge his or her dignity as a human being. According to the standard view, all persons are owed respect, even if one holds some of them in low esteem. I suspect that it is psychologically impossible fully to respect someone whom one holds in very low esteem. In any case, I am sure that very low self-esteem undermines self-respect.

20. Quoted in an Associated Press article by Jane See White, the *Home News*, New Brunswick, N.J., October 4, 1980.

21. Annual report of the National Advisory Council on Economic Opportunity, 1979, excerpted in the *American Federationist*, October 1979.

22. This need not be so in all societies. There could be and there have been societies where there is nothing like a job, as we know them, to be had. Persons would, I suppose, still have the need for a sense of themselves as productive, contributing members, but it would take different forms in different kinds of society.

Chapter Four

1. Maureen Hedgepeth in *Testimony*, a film produced by Harold Mayer and Lynne Rhodes Mayer for the National Citizens Committee for Justice for J. P. Stevens Workers.

2. Adoption of the resolution followed an independent investigation by an NCC committee which reviewed the court and National Labor Relations Board documents and interviewed representatives of both the union and the company. The report of this committee, a 1978 update, and the text of the resolution are printed in (NCC, 1978).

3. WOHRC Fact Sheet, March 1980.

4. Cotton textile mills had mushroomed in the South during the late nineteenth and early twentieth centuries, bringing industrialization to the South. The "industrial exodus" from New England, however, took place mainly in the post-World War II period. Historian Melton McLaurin argues that the "image of the Southern cotton textile worker as a docile and tractable laborer, was created and carefully cultivated by promoters of the New South, by state government agencies, and by mill owners and mill presidents" (McLaurin, 1971, xiii). He documents the labor struggles and organiz-

ing efforts that have occurred since the early days of the Southern textile industry (the first major strike, by the Knights of Labor, took place in Augusta, Georgia in 1886). These efforts belie the image of southern operatives as docile. At the same time, the mill owners' responses (evicting workers from company-owned housing, closing the company store when union activity was threatened—thus cutting workers and their families off from their only source of food—and maintaining tight control of every aspect of life in the mill villages) help to explain how the ways in which the mill village system was patterned after the southern plantation system have strengthened the hand of the mill owners in resisting the efforts of southern textile workers to organize and act collectively. (See McLaurin, 1971, Chapter 2, "The Industrial Plantation.")

5. For example, in 1914 Congress passed the Clayton Act which included a list of normal strike activities and forbade the federal courts to issue injunctions against them as long as they were done "peaceably" and "lawfully." But in 1921 the Supreme Court ruled that the Clayton Act said nothing new: it remained up to the courts to decide what constitutes "peaceable" and "lawful" activity (Reynolds, 1961, 125).

6. *Payne* v. *Western and Atlantic Railroad*, 81 Tenn. 507.519–20 (1884) (quoted and cited in Ladenson). This doctrine remains largely in effect today, subject to the following sorts of qualifications: 1) Specific legislation disallows dismissal (and other forms of discrimination) for specific reasons. For example, the Wagner Act prohibits such action by employers in retaliation for an employee's union activity; the OSH Act forbids such retaliation against an employee for filing a complaint with OSHA. Employers are still at liberty to permanently replace striking workers unless the strike is in response to employer unfair labor practices. 2) Most union contracts contain a clause requiring that dismissals be only for "just cause" (but recall that only some 23 percent of U.S. workers are covered by such contracts). 3) Where government acts as an employer, the Supreme Court ruled in *Pickering* v. *Bd of Ed.* it is required to respect the constitutional rights of employees (Ladenson, 1983). 4) Courts have occasionally upheld suits of fired employees on grounds of public policy. In general, though, they have treated an employer's right to discharge an employee as absolute. For example, in the case of a secretary fired for refusing to indicate falsely that she was not available for jury duty, the court acknowledged that the reason for her discharge was "quite reprehensible," but stated "her employer could discharge her with or without cause. . . . It makes no difference if the employer had a bad motive in so doing." (*Mallard* v. *Boring*, Cal. App. 2d. 390, 394, 6 Cal. Rptr. 171, 174 Ct. App. 1962; quoted in Ladenson, 1983.) There is, however, a recent decision by the Illinois Supreme Court (*Palmateer* v. *International Harvester Corp.*, 1981) which would greatly expand the protection of workers against unjust dismissal. The decision offers much broader and more general criteria than any previous rulings for invoking public policy to find a dismissal illegitimate. If followed by other courts, this decision could seriously undermine the doctrine of employment at will (Ladenson, 1983).

7. Informally called the Wagner Act, in reference to its sponsor, the 1935 National Labor Relations Act was extensively amended in 1947 by the Taft-Hartley Act (the Labor Management Relations Act), and by other less extensive amendments from time to time. The Act covers private employers engaged in interstate commerce involving $50,000 a year or more. Recently non-profit hospitals were added to its coverage. Due to broad federal powers to regulate commerce, almost all private and semi-private employers come under the Act. The main exceptions are public employees, airline and railroad employees (who are covered by the Railway Labor Act), agricultural and domestic workers, and independent contractors and supervisors. Public employees are covered under a wide range of federal, state and local laws.

8. For a critique of the tendency in labor relations theory and practice to interpret the Wagner Act as establishing a framework for industrial democracy, i.e., a system in which workplaces are governed jointly by workers (or their representatives) and management, and hence are appropriately viewed as small societies ruled with the consent of the governed, see Stone, 1981.

9. Some readers may find it apparently unfair or inconsistent of me to speak in at least implicitly disapproving tones, here and elsewhere, of employers disregarding, disobeying, and seeking to change the law while elsewhere I speak sympathetically, even approvingly of workers and their unions doing the same things. Recall that I do not claim, or aspire, to be neutral. I would, however, like, as far as possible to be both fair and consistent. While I believe there is a general moral obligation to obey the law in a just society, I have grave doubts about whether our society qualifies in some fundamental respects as just. Furthermore, I believe that even in an otherwise just society, it is sometimes permissible—and sometimes even morally obligatory—to disobey unjust laws, and take other measures in an effort to change them. On the other hand, of course, many actions which are perfectly legal are morally reprehensible, including seeking legal authorization for acts or arrangements which are unjust. Thus, in determining my moral attitude toward the actions and efforts of various individuals and groups, their legal status is the tail, not the dog. Indeed, in my view, the law in general, vis-à-vis not just moral evaluation but social and economic actions and conditions, tends to be the tail—albeit a tail that occasionally wags the dog.

10. A virtue, perhaps, to those who believe in the myth of rugged individualism, but contrary to the very logic of collective action that gives rise to the unionism.

11. The United Electrical Workers withheld dues payments to the CIO because of the CIO's failure to protect UE locals from raids by CIO unions whose officials had signed the anti-communist oath. UE disaffiliated from the CIO prior to being "expelled."

12. *Economic Notes*, Vol. 50, nos. 7–8, July–August 1982, p. 8. It is interesting that sympathy strikes and secondary boycotts are illegal in Canada also (Blanpain, 1977). That such an action was successfully carried out may be explained by two factors. First, labor in Canada, especially where it is fully organized, as in the auto industry, is politically more powerful than is the case in the U.S., and hence better able to protect itself against reprisals. Second, the fact that the primary and secondary activities took place in different countries would have made it difficult or impossible for J. P. Stevens to bring action against the Canadian workers. Sympathy strikes and other collective secondary actions are fully legal in many industrialized countries, for example, Great Britain, Italy, Sweden, and Denmark (Blanpain, 1977).

13. An important difference between union shop and agency shop is that the courts have generally found that mandatory agency shop fees may be charged to cover expenditures related to collective bargaining, contract administration and grievance adjustment, but not for any other union activities, such as political activities. This raises very knotty problems of determining which activities are related to collective bargaining and which are not. Unless one takes a very narrow view, almost any activity of a union is related to collective bargaining, for such factors as the climate of public opinion and the passage of labor-related legislation can have important impact on the course of negotiations, especially over the long term.

14. It was most important to those unions in industries where employment is brief, intermittent, or seasonal, such as construction and longshoring, since without the closed shop their members could repeatedly be subject to arbitrary or discriminatory treatment each time they sought new employment. This potentially serious problem appears to be handled reasonably well through agreements whereby employers hire new employees exclusively through the union hiring hall. Such agreements are legal "so long as there is neither a provision in the agreement nor a practice in effect that discriminates against nonunion members in favor of union members or otherwise discriminates on the basis of union membership obligations. Both the agreement and the actual operation of the hiring hall must be nondiscriminatory; referrals must be made without reference to union membership or irrelevant or arbitrary considerations such as race. Referral standards or procedures, even if nondiscriminatory on their face, are unlawful when they continue previously discriminatory conditions of referral. However, a union may in setting referral standards consider legitimate aims such as sharing available work and easing the impact of local unemployment. It may also

charge referral fees if the amount of the fee is reasonably related to the cost of operating the referral service" ("A Guide to Basic Law and Procedures under the National Labor Relations Act," p. 33).

15. Under the law, a union is always subject to decertification by vote of a majority of those in the bargaining unit, members and nonmembers.

16. Some philosophers have attempted to account for and justify such differences by distinguishing between rights and liberties on one hand and the *worth* to an individual of those rights and liberties on the other. (See, e.g., Rawls, 1971, 204.) Rawls claims that justice requires that the former, but not the latter, be equal. (He does, however, argue for a theoretically significant, but practically indeterminate, constraint on the economic inequalities that largely determine the relative worth of rights and liberties.) For a thoroughgoing critique of the assumption that personal and political equality (equal rights and liberties) is compatible with significant economic inequality (unequal worth of rights and liberties), see Norman Daniels, "Equal Liberty and Unequal Worth of Liberty" in Daniels, 1974, 253–81.

17. Robert Nozick asserts: "Taxation of earnings from labor is on a par with forced labor" (Nozick, 1974, 169). He goes on to say that this extends also to earnings from interest, entrepreneurial profits, and so on (Nozick, 1974, 170).

18. Would that we were less willing than we seem, in fact, to be.

19. Where children are or may be involved, we may be even more reluctant to allow a homeowner's imprudence, or selfishness, or poverty, to prevent their possible rescue.

20. In an election with more than two alternatives on the ballot, if no choice receives a majority, a run-off is held between the top two vote-getters. (The set of alternatives originally presented for balloting must include "No Union.")

21. Even libertarian philosopher Robert Nozick says that, when the liberty of individuals to engage in certain activities is justifiably restricted, it is not always necessary to compensate them—either by providing funds for them to obtain the goods or services the restricted activity would have afforded them or by providing substitute goods or services without charge. Such compensation must be provided, he says, only in the event that, and to the extent that, the individual is *disadvantaged* by the restriction (Nozick, 1974, 78–84, 110–13). He offers no satisfactory account of what distinguishes activities he thinks may justifiably be restricted (examples he offers include fending for oneself by acting to punish those who violate one's rights, in the presence of a government which takes responsibility for adjudicating disputes and punishing violators; driving a car while in a medical condition that makes driving especially dangerous to others; and using a very risky but profitable manufacturing process) from those he thinks may not justifiably be restricted (which presumably would include fending for oneself in the presence of a majority-elected union in one's bargaining unit). Nor does he offer an adequate account of what constitutes being disadvantaged by a prohibition. He says that, in an automobile dependent society, the individual prohibited from driving must be compensated, e.g., by being provided funds for taxi service or taxi service itself to enable him or her to live a normal life. But the cost he or she *would have* incurred owning and driving a car may be deducted from the monetary compensation, or charged for the in-kind compensation. (Moreover, if the individual were independently wealthy and could pay for alternative transportation without hardship, no compensation need be provided.) In contrast, he sees not even a *prima facie* case for compensation in the case of the manufacturing process. He says: "If some person wishes to use a very risky but efficient (and if things go well *harmless*) process in manufacturing a product, must the residents near the factory compensate him for the economic loss he suffers from not being allowed to use the possibly dangerous process? Surely not." (Nozick, 1974, 79. Emphasis in original.) My intuitions agree with Nozick's on these two examples, but he offers no theoretical account or justification for drawing the line where he does, hence no principle to appeal to in deciding cases, such as union security, where intuitions diverge. In any event, on the second question, that of whether the individual is disadvantaged, it seems plausible to say that the dues

structure in effect in most unions reasonably ensures that an individual required to pay dues is not disadvantaged—especially when we consider that in "fending for him- or herself" the independent would, willy, nilly, be advantaged by the presence of the union.

With regard to persons prohibited from fending for themselves by punishing those who violate their rights, Nozick says that they must be provided with protective services, and some may have to be provided those services at a fee that is less than the cost of the services (because fending for themselves would have cost them less and it would be a hardship for them to pay the full fee). Still, says Nozick, "These persons may, of course, choose to refuse to pay the fee and so do without these compensatory services" (Nozic, 1974, 113). This would be analogous to allowing exclusive representation but denying the duty of fair representation that is generally accepted as its corollary. It is both practically unfeasible and morally repugnant to tell people that they may not act in their own behalf *and* no one is bound to act for them. Thus the only equitable solution is to require fair representation and require those who can to pay their share of the cost.

22. I do not mean to suggest that elimination of discrimination for the future, even if it were fully achieved, would be an adequate response to the need to rectify the results of generations of discrimination in the past. Employers and unions—especially but not exclusively those which have engaged in or cooperated with discriminatory practices in the past—have an obligation to devise effective means to hasten the elimination of racial and sexual segregation and ghettoization of the workforce. Unions could play a positive role by making an explicit effort to achieve an equitable distribution of jobs (especially where hiring halls are used) and by making special efforts to include members of previously excluded groups in apprenticeship programs. Thus the need to rectify past discrimination does not count against the union hiring hall as a form of union security.

23. While these provisions appear to dispose of the present argument, one may question whether, in another respect, they don't go too far. If the idea of union security is to be more than a mere legalism, it may be argued, unions need the power to protect themselves against persons who are intent on betraying and, if possible, destroying them.

24. Special legislation, the Railway Labor Act, covers railroad and airline employees. Also, although the postal service is now defined as a quasi-private employer, and its employees are covered by the NLRA, postal workers are, nevertheless, prohibited from striking and must sign a no-strike pledge to be hired. It should be noted that both the Taft-Hartley Act and the Railway Labor Act contain strike control measures that can be initiated by the President of the United States if he or she deems a strike situation to constitute a national emergency. These provisions are controversial at best. Unfortunately, space does not permit us to examine them here. For discussion, see Cullen, 1968.

25. In 1950, one in every 7.5 (non-agricultural) employees in the U.S. was a government worker; in 1981, the figure was one in every 5.7 (*Monthly Labor Review*, January 1983, 77). In view of all we have heard recently about the "bloated" federal bureaucracy and payroll, it is interesting to note that, between 1950 and 1981, the total (non-agricultural) paid labor force doubled and the number of state and local government workers quadrupled, while the number of federal government employees increased by less than 50 percent (*Monthly Labor Review*, January 1983, 77).

26. Strikers are protected against being permanently replaced only if the strike is in protest against an unfair labor practice (i.e., an action that is illegal under the Wagner Act) by the employer. Even in such "protected" strikes, the employer may temporarily replace striking workers and keep the plant operating. (It could be argued that employers ought to be forbidden to replace striking workers at all, even if it means they must cease operations for the duration of a strike—as they are, for example, in Italy, Sweden, and Quebec (Blanpain, 1977). This position may be supported on the grounds that, *given* the compelling case for the right to strike, such a policy would help

to prevent union-busting by employers and bitter picketline confrontations between strikers and strikebreakers, with the suffering and potential for violence inherent in such situations. There seems to be little prospect that such a policy will be adopted in the U.S. in the near future, and we shall not discuss it further here.)

27. For many of these arguments and responses, I rely on Aboud and Aboud, 1974.

28. The federal government has successfully appealed to sovereign immunity as a defense against suits charging the government with negligence in exposing shipyard workers and their families to asbestos during World War II (*New York Times*, September 18, 1982, 36).

29. A third kind of third-party procedure is fact-finding. A fact-finder investigates a dispute and issues a report which usually contains recommendations for resolution. Unlike a mediator's suggestions, which are generally unpublicized, a fact-finder's report is usually made public in an effort to bring pressure on the parties to accept its recommendations. Since fact-finding, like mediation, does not bind the parties, it does not guarantee a way out of impasse.

30. U.S. unions which call themselves "international" do so because they have, or lay claim to, members in Canada.

31. For an excellent and informative discussion of the role of participation in alternative theories of democracy, and of the implications of the available empirical evidence for those theories, see Pateman, 1970.

Chapter Five

1. I think of the views sketched here as essentially Marxian in the sense that they are inspired by what I take to be fundamental aspects of Marx's views. I make no attempt, in general, to show that what I say can be supported by, much less derived from, Marx's texts.

An excellent paper articulating views that are in many ways close to mine is Ruth Anna Putnam's "Rights of Persons and the Liberal Tradition" (Putnam, 1975). Perhaps the biggest difference between our views is that I believe rights will be with us, and have important work to do, for quite some time to come, while she appears to believe that they are at or near the end of their useful existence. On this point, her view seems closer than mine to Marx's. I suspect that this may be because each of them wrote during a period (one more short-lived than the other) when fundamental change in the societies of the United States or Western Europe in the near future appeared far more likely than is the case today.

Related to this point are two likely challenges to the appropriateness of calling my views Marxian at all. These challenges focus on the fact that I take seriously, first, moral ideas and arguments in general, and, second, rights in particular. The first challenge claims that the theory of the mature, "scientific" Marx was not normative or evaluative at all, so at most I could claim to be inspired by the early, "humanistic" Marx (see Althusser, 1969, 34ff and 51–86). The short response to this challenge is that I reject the "two Marxes" thesis. I shall not attempt a longer response here.

The second challenge maintains that, granted that Marx's mature work has evaluative content, he had no use for juridical concepts such as those of rights and justice (see Wood, 1972, and Tucker, 1969, 37–53). This view has, I believe, been convincingly refuted (see Holmstrom, 1977, 366–8; Husami, 1978; and Buchanan, 1982, Chapter 4). Still, there remains the fact that Marx himself not only avoided using the terminology of rights and justice, he also referred to them as "ideas which in a certain period had some meaning but have now become obsolete verbal rubbish," and as "ideological nonsense" (Marx, 1875, 531). As I suggested above, this may be in part because he viewed revolutionary change as imminent, and thus believed that the circumstances giving rise to the need for such concepts would soon be eliminated. No doubt he also believed that use of these concepts could be misleading, since it might be taken to imply that, with the correction of a few abuses, capitalism could be rendered fair or just. For reasons that will emerge below, I believe that this is a risk that must be taken.

2. Compare Karl Marx: "But the human essence is no abstraction inherent in each single individual. In its reality it is the ensemble of the social relations" ("These on Feuerbach," No. VI (Marx, 1845, 145)).

3. On the historical development of the concept and language of rights, see for example Golding, 1978; Kamenka 1978a; Minogue, 1978.

4. Recall Rawls's distinction between rights and liberties on one hand and the *worth* of rights and liberties on the other (Chapter Four, note 16).

5. In a later "postscript" Feinbert says:

In fact, the poor benighted citizens of Nowheresville do have various rights, whether they know it or not. They could not possible know—or understand—that they have rights, however, because they do not even have the *concept* of a personal right. Such a notion has never even been dreamed of in Nowheresville. The inhabitants are consequently deficient in respect for self and others. [Feinberg, 1978, 32]

6. This point is more fully developed by Katheryn Pyne Addelson in her paper, "Respect" (unpublished).

7. Compare Ronald Dworkin's "Can Rights be Controversial?" (Dworkin, 1978, 279–90).

8. For more on the distinction between internal and external criticisms, see Buchanan, 1982, chap. 4.

References

Aboud, A., and G. Aboud. 1974. *The Right to Strike in Public Employment*. New York State School of Industrial and Labor Relations, Ithaca: Cornell University Press.

Addelson, K. P. "Respect" (unpublished).

Althusser, L. 1969. *For Marx*. New York: Pantheon.

American Federationist. October 1979.

Anderson, J. M. 1979. *Occupational Lung Disease*. American Lung Association (no place of publication given).

Bandman, E., and B. Bandman, eds. 1978. *Bioethics and Human Rights*. Boston: Little Brown.

Barnet, R. J., and R. E. Miller. 1974. *Global Reach: The Power of the Multi-National Corporations*. New York: Simon and Schuster.

Bedeau, H. A. 1971. *Justice and Equality*. Englewood Cliffs: Prentice Hall.

Ben-Horin, D. 1979. "The Sterility Scandal." *Mother Jones* (May): 51–63.

Berlin, I. 1958. *Two Concepts of Liberty* (Inaugural Lecture). Revised form reprinted in Berlin, 1969; excerpt reprinted in Dewey and Gould, 1970. (References in the text are to Dewey and Gould, 1970.)
———. 1969. *Four Essays on Liberty*. London: Oxford University Press.

Berman, D. M. 1978. *Death on the Job: Occupational Health and Safety Struggles in the United States*. New York: Monthly Review Press.

Bertin, J. E. 1982. Testimony at hearings on "Genetic Screening and the Handling of High Risk Groups in the Workplace," before the Subcommittee on Investigations and Oversight of the Committee on Science and Technology, U. S. House of Representatives, October 14, 15, 1981. Washington, DC: U. S. Government Printing Office.

Blanpain, R. 1977. *International Encyclopedia for Labor Law and Industrial Relations*. Deventer, The Netherlands: Kluwer. (Updated periodically.)

Bosch, R. van den. 1980. *The Pesticide Conspiracy*. New York: Anchor Books.

Boyer, R. O., and H. M. Morais. 1972. *Labor's Untold Story*. 3rd. ed.

New York: United Electrical Radio and Machine Workers of America (U.E.).

Boyle, J. M., Jr. 1980. "Toward Understanding the Principle of Double Effect." *Ethics* 90, no. 4: 527–38.

Bowles, S., and H. Gintis. 1976. *Schooling in Capitalist America: Educational Reform and the Contradictions of Economic Life.* New York: Basic Books.

Braverman, H. 1974. *Labor and Monopoly Capital.* New York: Monthly Review Press.

Brenner, M. H. 1976. *Estimating the Social Costs of National Economic Policy: Implications for Mental and Physical Health and Clinical Aggression.* Report for the Joint Economic Committee of Congress. Washington, DC: U. S. Government Printing Office.

Brodeur, P. 1974. *Expendable Americans.* New York: the Viking Press.

Buchanan, A. 1978. "Medical Paternalism." *Philosophy & Public Affairs* 7, no. 4: 370–90.

———. 1982. *Marx and Justice: The Radical Critique of Liberalism.* Totowa, NJ: Rowman and Littlefield.

Burton, J. F., and C. Krider. 1972. "The Role and Consequences of Strikes by Public Employees." In J. J. Lowenberg and M. H. Moskow, eds., *Collective Bargaining in Government.* Englewood Cliffs: Prentice Hall. (Cited in Aboud and Aboud, 1974.)

CACOSH Health & Safety News. 1979. Vol. 6, no. 8. Chicago: The Chicago Area Committee on Occupational Safety & Health (CACOSH).

Chamberlain, N. W. 1972. "Public vs. Private Sector Bargaining." In Lowenberg and Moskow, 1972 (quoted in Aboud and Aboud).

CLUW News. Fall, 1979. Coalition of Labor Union Women, New York.

Cobb, S. and S. Kasl. 1977. *Termination: The Consequences of Job Loss.* DHEW (NIOSH) Publication No. 77–224. Washington, DC: U.S. Government Printing Office. (Cited in *Economic Dislocation.*)

Cohen, G. 1978. "Robert Nozick and Wilt Chamberlain: How Patterns Preserve Liberty." In Arthur and Shaw, ed., *Justice and Economic Distributions.* Englewood Cliffs: Prentice Hall. Pp. 246–62.

———. 1979. "Capitalism, Freedom and the Proletariat," In Alan Ryan, ed., *The Idea of Freedom: Essays in Honor of Isaiah Berlin.* Oxford: Oxford University Press.

———. 1983. "The Structure of Proletarian Unfreedom." *Philosophy & Public Affairs* 12, no. 1: 3–33.

Cronin, J. B. 1971. "Cause and Effect? Investigations into Aspects of Industrial Accidents in the United Kingdom." *International Labour Review* 103, no. 2: 99–115. (Cited in Sass, 1977.)

Cullen, D. E. 1968. *National Emergency Strikes*. New School of Industrial and Labor Relations. Ithaca: Cornell University Press.

Daily Record. 1979. Northwest New Jersey, April 1.

Daily World. February 28, 1980.

Daniels, N., ed. 1974. *Reading Rawls*. New York: Basic Books.

DeCarvalho, P., A. Heitzer, J. Meyer, B. Zack Quindel, M. Goldstein Robbins, M. Robbins, and J. Williamson. 1981. *Plant Closings and Runaway Industries: Strategies for Labor*. Washington, DC: National Labor Law Center.

DeGeorge, R., and J. A. Pichler, eds. 1978. *Ethics, Free Enterprise and Public Policy*. New York: Oxford University Press.

Dewey, R. E., and J. A. Gould, eds. 1970. *Freedom: Its History, Nature and Varieties*. New York: The Macmillan Co.

Dreier, P. 1980. "Plant Closings Are Good Business, but Bad News." *In These Times*, Feb. 13-19, p. 18.

Dworkin, G. 1971. "Paternalism." In Richard A. Wasserstrom, ed., *Morality and the Law*. Belmont, CA: Wadsworth Publishing Co.

Dworkin, R. 1978. *Taking Rights Seriously*. Cambridge, MA: Harvard University Press.

Economic Dislocation: Plant Closings, Plant Relocations and Plant Conversions. 1979. Joint Report of Labor Union Study Tour Participants (UAW, USWA, IAM).

Economic Notes. 1979. Vol. 47, nos. 4–5, New York: Labor Research Association.

———. 1980. Vol. 48, no. 5.

———. 1982. Vol. 50, nos. 7-8.

Eisner, E. G., and I. P. Sipser, 1970. "The Charleston Hospital Dispute: Organizing Public Employees and the Right to Strike." *St. John's Law Review* 45, no. 2 (Dec.): 254–72.

Elkiss, H. 1981. "Hazardous Work and Employee Rights: Can OSHA Protect Those Who Protect Themselves?" *Labor Studies Journal* 6, no. 1: 68–81.

Epstein, S. S. 1979. *The Politics of Cancer*. New York: Anchor Books.

Federal Register. 1980. Vol. 45, no. 23 (Feb. 1): 7514–17.

———. Vol. 45, no. 102 (May 23).

Feinberg, J. 1970. "The Nature and Value of Rights." *The Journal of Value Inquiry* 4, pp. 243–57. Reprinted in Bandman and Bandman, 1978; in Lyons, 1979; and in Feinberg, 1980. (Page references in the text are to Lyons, 1979.)

———. 1978. "A Postscript to the Nature and Value of Rights, (1977)." In Bandman and Bandman, 1978.

———. 1980. *Rights, Justice, and the Bounds of Liberty*. Princeton: Princeton University Press.

Fowler, M. 1982. "Coercion and Practical Reason." *Social Theory and Practice* 8, no. 83: 329–55.

Frankfurt, H. 1973. "Coercion and Moral Responsibility." In T. Honderich, 1976.

Fried, C. 1981. *Contract as Promise.* Cambridge, MA: Harvard University Press.

Golding, M. P. 1978. "The Concept of Rights: A Historical Sketch." In Bandman and Bandman, 1978.

Goldman, A. H. 1980. *The Moral Foundations of Professional Ethics.* Totowa, NJ: Rowman and Littlefield.

Gotbaum, V. 1978. "Public Service Strikes: Where Prevention Is Worse than the Cure." In DeGeorge and Pichler, 1978.

The Guardian. July 1, 1981.

Hampden-Turner, C. 1973. "The Factory as an Oppressive and Non-Emancipatory Environment." In Hunnius, Garson, and Case, eds., 1973.

Hansen, H. C. 1980. "Pro and Con: Should Public Servants Have the Right to Strike?" *Family Weekly,* July 13.

Hanslowe, K. L. 1967. *The Emerging Law of Labor Relations in Public Employment.* New York State School of Industrial and Labor Relations. Ithaca: Cornell University Press. (quoted in Eisner and Sipser, 1970.)

Holmstrom, N. 1977. "Exploitation." *Canadian Journal of Philosophy* 7, no. 2: 353–69.

The Home News. 1979. New Brunswick, NJ. January 3.

———. 1980. New Brunswick, NJ. February 27.

———. 1980. New Brunswick, NJ. October 4.

Honderich, T., ed. 1976. *Social Ends and Political Means.* London: Routledge and Kegan Paul.

Hume, D. 1739. *A Treatise of Human Nature.* 2nd ed. Ed. L. A. Selby-Bigge, Oxford: Oxford University Press, 1978.

Hunnius, G., G. D. Garson, and J. Case, eds. 1973. *Workers' Control.* New York: Random House.

Husami, Z. 1978. "Marx on Distributive Justice." *Philosophy & Public Affairs* 8, no. 1: 27–64.

In These Times. March 12–25, 1980.

———. April 2–8, 1980.

Kamenka, E. 1978. "The Anatomy of an Idea." In Kamenka and Erh-Soon Tay eds., 1978.

Kamenka, E., and A. Erh-Soon Tay eds. 1978. *Human Rights.* London: Edward Arnold.

Kaye, H. 1979. "Deaths on the Job—A Nationwide Crisis." *Daily World.* March 15, pp. 1, 22.

Kornhauser, A. 1965. *Mental Health of the Industrial Worker: A Detroit Study.* New York: John Wiley & Sons.

Labor Update. 1981. Washington DC: National Labor Law Center. May.

Ladenson, R. F. 1983. *A Philosophy of Free Expression.* Totowa, NJ: Rowman & Allanheld.

Laslett, P., and G. Runciman, eds. 1962. *Philosophy, Politics and Society.* Ser. 2. London: Basil Blackwell.

Lehmann, P. (n.d.) "Protecting Women Out of Their Jobs." Somerville, MA: New England Free Press. (pamphlet)

Lerner, J. (n.d.) *Too Many Hours!: Labor's Struggle to Shorten the Work Day.* New York: United Electrical, Radio and Machine Workers of America.

LOHP Monitor. 1979. Vol. 7, no. 3 Berkeley: Labor Occupational Health Program (LOHP), University of California Center for Labor Research and Education.

——. 1980. Vol. 8, no. 2

——. 1981. Vol. 9, no. 2

LOHP Pesticide Fact Sheet. 1979. Berkeley: Labor Occupational Health Program (LOHP), University of California Center for Labor Research and Education.

Lowenberg, J. J., and M. H. Moskow, eds. 1972. *Collective Bargaining in Government.* Englewood Cliffs: Prentice Hall.

Lyons, D. 1975. "Welcome Threats and Coercive Offers." *Philosophy* 50, pp. 425–36.

——, ed. 1979. *Rights.* Belmont, CA: Wadsworth Publishing Co.

Male, R. 1965. "Labor Crises and the Role of Management." In *Developments in Public Employee Relations.* (Cited in Eisner and Sipser, 1970.)

Marx, K. 1843. "On the Jewish Question." In Tucker, 1978.

——. 1845. "Theses on Feuerbach." In Tucker, 1978.

——. 1875. "Critique of the Gotha Program." In Tucker, 1978.

Mayer, H., and L. Rhodes Mayer. 1976. *Testimony,* a film produced for the National Citizens Committee for Justice for J. P. Stevens Workers.

McLaurin, M. 1971. *Paternalism and Protest: Southern Cotton Mill Workers and Organized Labor, 1875–1905.* Westport: Greenwood Publishing Corp.

Meissner, M. 1971. "The Long Arm of the Job: A Study of Work and Leisure." *Industrial Relations* 10, no. 3: 239–60.

Milkman, R. 1980. "Organizing the Sexual Division of Labor: Historical Perspectives on 'Women's Work' and the American Labor Movement." *Socialist Review* 49, pp. 95–150.

Mill, J. S. 1859. *On Liberty.* Ed. D. Spitz, New York: W. W. Norton, 1975.

Minogue, K. R. 1978. "Natural Rights, Ideology, and the Game of Life." In Kamenka and Erh-Soon Tay, eds., 1978.

Monthly Labor Review. January 1983.

Murray, T. H. 1983. "Warning: Screening Workers for Genetic Risk." *The Hastings Center Report.* Vol 13, no 1: 5–8. Hastings-on-Hudson: The Hastings Center Institute of Society, Ethics and the Life Sciences.

NACLA. 1978. "Dying for Work, Occupational Health and Asbestos." *NACLA Report on the Americas* 12 no. 2. March/April.

NCC. 1978. *Fabric of Injustice: The Struggle at J. P. Stevens.* 2nd rev. ed. The National Council of the Churches of Christ in the U.S.A.

The New York Times. 1982. Barnaby J. Feder, "Paying Asbestos Damages, Government's Liability Questioned." September 18, pp. 35–36.

NJCOSH Newsletter. May 1979. Clark, NJ: New Jersey Committee for Occupational Safety and Health (NJCOSH).

NLRB. 1978. "A guide to Basic Law and Procedures Under the National Labor Relations Act." Washington, DC: U. S. Government Printing Office.

———. 1980. *Forty-Fifth Annual Report of the National Labor Relations Board.* Washington, DC: U. S. Government Printing Office.

Nozick, R. 1969. "Coercion." In *Philosophy, Science and Method.* Ed. S. Morgenbesser, *et al.* New York: St. Martin's Press.

———. 1974. *Anarchy, State, and Utopia.* New York: Basic Books.

Nothstein, G. Z. 1981. *The Law of Occupational Safety and Health.* New York: The Free Press.

Pateman, C. 1970. *Participation and Democratic Theory.* London: Cambridge University Press.

Pennock, J. R., and J. W. Chapman, eds. 1972. *Coercion.* Vol. 14 of NOMOS series. Chicago/New York: Aldrine-Atherton.

Putnam, R. A. 1976. "Rights of Persons and the Liberal Tradition." In Honderich, 1976.

Rawls, J. 1971. *A Theory of Justice.* Cambridge: Harvard University Press.

Rayback, J. G. 1966. *A History of American Labor.* 2nd ed. New York: The Macmillan Co.

Reynolds, L. G. 1961. *Labor Economics and Labor Relations.* 3rd ed. Englewood Cliffs: Prentice Hall.

Safer Times. 1978. Philadelphia: Philadelphia Area Committee on Occupational Safety & Health (PHILAPOSH). July/August.

Sandel, M. 1982. *Liberalism and the Limits of Justice*, Cambridge: Cambridge University Press.

Saso, C. D. 1970. *Coping With Public Employee Strikes*. Chicago: Public Personnel Association. (Quoted in Aboud and Aboud.)

Sass, R. 1977. "Work at the Centre." *Hazards at Work: Law and the Workplace*. Proceedings of a national seminar, Toronto, Canada, November 16–17.

Schwartz, A. 1982. "Meaningful Work." *Ethics* 92, no. 4, (July): 634–46.

———. 1981. "Against Universality." *The Journal of Philosophy*. 78, no. 3 (March): 127–43.

———. "The Possibility of Autonomy" (unpublished).

Scott, R. 1974. *Muscle and Blood*. New York: E. P. Dutton.

Sennett, R., and J. Cobb. 1973. *The Hidden Injuries of Class*. New York: Random House.

Severo, R. 1980. "Genetic Tests by Industry Raise Questions on Rights of Workers." *The New York Times*, February 3, pp. 1, 36.

Sheraton World. 1979. Vol 11, no. 4. Boston: The Sheraton Corporation.

Shue, H. 1980. *Basic Rights*. Princeton: Princeton University Press.

Spencer, C. 1977. *Blue Collar: An Internal Examination of the Workplace*. Chicago: Lakeside Charter Books.

Spero, S. 1948. *The Government as Employer*. (Quoted in Eisner and Sipser, 1970.)

Staub, S. March 1978. "Point/Counterpoint." *Instructor*. Reprinted and distributed by the National Right to Work Committee, Fairfax, Va.

Stellman, J. M. 1977. *Women's Work, Women's Health*, Pantheon Books, New York.

Stellman, J. M., and S. Daum. 1973. *Work Is Dangerous to Your Health*. New York: Random House.

Stone, K. V. W. 1981. "The Post-War Paradigm in American Labor Law." *The Yale Law Journal*. 90, no. 7: 1509–80.

Terkel, Studs. 1974. *Working: People Talk About What They Do All Day and How They Feel About What They Do*. New York: Random House.

Tucker, R. C. 1969. *The Marxian Revolutionary Idea*. New York: W. W. Norton.

———. 1978. *The Marx-Engles Reader*. 2nd ed. New York: W. W. Norton.

VanDeVeer, D. 1980. "The Contractual Argument for Withholding Medical Information." *Philosophy & Public Affairs* 9, no. 2: 198–205.

Weisenfeld, A. 1969. "Public Employees Are Still Second-Class Citizens." *Labor Law Journal*. 20. (Cited in Eisner and Sipser, 1970.)

Wellington, H. H., and R. K. Winter. 1969. "The Limits of Collective Bargaining in Public Employment." *Yale Law Journal* 77: 1107–27. (Quoted in Aboud and Aboud, 1974.)

Williams, B. A. O. 1962. "The Idea of Equality." In Laslett and Runciman, 1962; reprinted in Bedau, 1971. (References in the text are to Bedau, 1971.)

Witt, M., and S. Early. "The Worker as Safety Inspector." *Working Papers* 7, no. 5 (Sept.-Oct. 1980): 21–29.

WOHRC Fact Sheet. 1980. New York: Columbia University, Women's Occupational Health Resource Center (WOHRC).

WOHRC NEWS. 1979. Vol. 1, no. 3. New York: Columbia University, Women's Occupational Health Resource Center (WOHRC).

———. 1980. Vol. 2, no. 1

———. 1980. Vol. 2, no. 2

———. 1983. Vol. 5, no. 1

Wood, A. 1972. "The Marxian Critique of Justice." *Philosophy & Public Affairs* 1, no. 3: 244–82.

Work in America. 1973. Report of a Special Task Force to the Secretary of Health, Education, and Welfare. Cambridge, MA: M.I.T. Press.

Wright, M. J. 1979. "Reproductive Hazards and 'Protective' Discrimination." *Feminist Studies* 5, no. 2: 302–9.

Zimmerman, D. 1981. "Coercive Wage Offers." *Philosophy & Public Affairs*. 10, no. 2 (Spring): 121–45.

Index

Access, right of, 44–48. *See also* Right-to-know
Accident, lost-time, 42–43
Acclimatization to hot environment, 60–61
Affidavit, non-communist, 96–97
Agency shop, 98
Agent Orange, 32, 33
Agricultural workers, 31
Allied Chemical Corporation, 67
American Civil Liberties Union, 12, 27
American Cyanamid Corporation case, 5–27; exclusionary policies, 5–7, 20–26; lead poisoning, 7–8, 19; protective and paternalistic policies, 15–20, 24–25; reproductive and privacy rights, 10–14; update, 26–27
American Textile Manufacturers Institute, 90
Anderson, J. Marion, 40
Arbitration, compulsory binding, 118–20
Armed forces employees, 32
Association of Federal, State, County, and Municipal Employees (AFSCME), 109–10
Autonomy, ideal of, 85–86, 127

Berlin, Isaiah, 126–28
Bertin, Joan, 12
Bingham, Eula, 26, 41
Boycotts, 88–89, 97–98
Brennan, William, 90
Brenner, Harvey, 83
Brown lung disease, 89–90
Buchanan, Allen, 134
Burnside Foundry case, 57–86; OSHA response to, 58, 68–69; right-to-a-job issue, 57, 75–84; right-to-refuse issue, 57, 61–74; steel industry hazards, 58–61
Byssinosis, 89–90

Carbon monoxide hazards, 59
Chamberlain, Neil W., 108

Child labor, 31, 32
Civil Rights Act, Title VII of, 10, 27
Closed shop, 98
Closings, plant. *See* Plant closings
Coalition for the Reproductive Rights of Workers (CRROW), 24
Coercion, 13–14
Coke oven workers, 59–60
Communism, unions and, 96–97
Company doctors. *See* Doctors, company
Compulsory binding arbitration, 118–20
Concerned Educators Against Forced Unionism, 103
Conflicting rights, 136–37, 140
Constitutional rights, 129
Contracts: employment, 13, 62–63; union, 65
Cost-benefit studies, OSHA, 9–10, 90
Cottle, Thomas, 83
Court injunction, 91–92, 108
Courts, recognition of rights through, 134–35. *See also* Supreme Court
"Critique of the Gotha Program" (Marx), 137
Critiques, external and internal, 140–41

DBCP (dibromochlorpropane), 29, 33, 36–39
Deering-Millikan Corporation, 93
Democracy: liberty rights and, 126–28; in unions, 121–22
Department of Health, Education and Welfare, 11
Dewey, Thomas, 108
Discrimination: in exclusionary policies, 10, 23–24; in protective policies, 15, 17, 19–20, 23–24; by unions, 104–6
Dismissal, threat of, 75–76
Doctors, company: communication of medical information by, 51–52; conflict of interest for, 43, 44–47; lack of occupational medicine education of, 49
Double effect, principle of, 34–36

Dow Chemical Company, 44
Dust, silica, 59
Dworkin, Gerald, 15–20, 53
Dworkin, Ronald, 110, 113, 132

Economic feasibility studies, 9–10
Eminent domain doctrine, 81
Employment contract, 13, 62–63
Equal Employment Opportunity Com-
    mission, 6
Equal rights, notion of, 137–39
Essentiality of government services, 111–
    14; of firefighters and police, 116–17
Exclusionary policies, 5–7, 20–26; discrim-
    ination in, 10, 23–24; guidelines for jus-
    tification of, 24
Exclusive representation, 103–4
Executive Order No. 11246, 10
External critiques, 140–41

Fair Labor Standards Act of 1938, 31
Feinberg, Joel, 132–33
Final-offer arbitration, 119–20
Firefighters: essentiality of services of,
    116–17; right to strike, 116–20
Food chain, 30
Formal rights, 128–31
Freedom, concepts of, 126–31
Free-rider issue, 101–3

Genetic screening, trend toward, 22–23
Gotbaum, Victor, 113
Government services, essentiality of, 111–
    14; of firefighters and police, 116–17
Grievance procedures, 62–63

Hampden-Turner, Charles, 84–85
Hansen, Hugh C., 110
Harassment, employer, 87–89
Harrison, Bennett, 77
Hazards. *See* Occupational hazards
Health, mental, 83–86
Health and Human Services (H & HS), 11,
    13
Heat stress, 60
Hoover, Herbert, 108
"Human rights," 124
Hume, David, 139

"Imminent danger," 66–67, 74
Incentive programs, 65–66, 69
Informed consent: necessary conditions
    for, 74–75; notion of, 13–14, 36–37, 55;
    right-to-know and, 28, 33; right-to-
    refuse and, 57, 63–64; sterilization with-
    out, 34–38

Injunction, court, 91–92, 108
Internal critique, 140–41
International Association of Machinists
    (IAM), 95
Investment decisions, company, 77–81

J. P. Stevens Company, 87–94; boycott of,
    88–89; response to unionization efforts,
    87–89, 105–06; right to strike and, 93–94;
    textile industry hazards, 89–91
Job, right-to-a-, 57, 75–84; as property
    right, 76–84
Justice, concept of, 139

Kornhauser, Arthur, 85, 86

Labeling requirements, 40–41, 43
Labor-Management Reporting and Dis-
    closure Act of 1959 (LMRDA), 121
Landrum-Griffin Act, 97, 121
Layoffs, 78–79
Lead poisoning, 7–8, 19
Legal rights, 9, 124, 134–35
Legal sovereignty, 109
Liberalism and the Limits of Justice (Sandel),
    133
Libertarianism, 101
Liberty, concepts of, 126–31
Lindley, James, 29
Lost-time accident, 42–43
Lyons, David, 135

Maintenance-of-membership, 98
Marshall, David, 58
Marx, Karl, 137–39
McLaurin, M., 105
"Meaningful Work" (Schwartz), 85
Mediation, 117–18
Medical departments, corporate, 43–45.
    See also Doctors, company
Medical records, privacy rights and, 45–48
Medicine, occupational, 49
Mental health, 83–86
Mill, John Stuart, 15
Monitoring records, 47
Moral rights, 8–9, 124, 125–26
Motivation: behind paternalism 17–19
Murray, Thomas, 44

National Association of Farmworkers Or-
    ganizations, 31
National Association of Manufacturers,
    95–96
National Council of Churches (NCC), 88–
    89
National Employment Priorities Act, 79

National Institute for Occupational Safety and Health (NIOSH), 40–41, 49
National Labor Relations Act of 1935, 71–72, 106
National Labor Relations Board (NLRB), 92–93
National Labor Relations Board v. Jones and Laughlin Steel Company, 93
National Right to Work Committee, 103
"Natural rights," 124
"Nature and Value of Rights, The" (Feinberg), 132
Needs, fundamental, 131, 139
Negligence, violation of rights by, 38
Noise hazards, 89
Non-communist affidavit, 96–97
Norris-LaGuardia Act of 1932, 92
Nozick, Robert, 127

Occidental Chemical Corporation case, 28–56; pesticides, 29, 30–31; right-to-know issue, 39–55; self-determination right, 55–56; reproductive hazard in, 28–29, 33–39
Occupational hazards: labeling requirement, 40–41, 43; lead poisoning, 7–8, 19; OSHA response to, 66–69; pesticides, 29, 30–31; posting requirement, 41–42, 43; reproductive, 19–21, 28–29, 33–39; in steel industry, 58–61; in textile industry, 89–91
Occupational health research, 43–44
Occupational medicine, 49
Occupational Safety and Health Act, 9–10
Occupational Safety and Health Administration (OSHA): Burnside Foundry and, 58, 68–69; cost-benefit studies of, 9–10, 90; labeling standard, 41; response to safety hazards, 7, 66–69
Occupational Safety and Health Review Commission, 26–27
Oil, Chemical and Atomic Workers Union (OCAW), 5, 27, 29, 67
Olin Corporation, 27
On Liberty (Mill), 15
Open shop, 98
OSHA. *See* Occupational Safety and Health Administration
O'Toole, Donald, 96

Partial work stoppages, 117
Paternalism, 15–20, 24–25; justification of, 15–18; motivation behind, 17–19; withholding information and, 51, 53–55
"Paternalism" (Dworkin), 15
Pesticides, 29, 30–31

Picciano, Dange J., 44
Plant closings, 76–81; solutions to, 94–95; worker-community takeover after, 80–81
Poisoning, lead, 7–8, 19
Police: essentiality of services of, 116–17; right to strike of, 116–20
Political process, public sector strikes and, 111, 114–16
Political sovereignty, 109
Posting requirements, 41–42, 43
Privacy Protection Study Commission, 46
Privacy rights, 10–14; medical records and, 45–48; monitoring records and, 47
Property right, job as, 76–84
Protective policies, 15–20, 23–24
Public sector: essentiality of services of, 111–14; market forces in, 114–15; preservation of political process in, 111, 114–16; recipients of services of, 114; right to strike in, 106–21
Putnam, Ruth Ann, 133

Rayback, Joseph, 93, 94
Refuse, right to. *See* Right-to-refuse
Regulations: Department of Labor, 22; OSH Act, 7, 9–10, 72–73; on sterilization programs, 11
Rehabilitation Act of 1973, 22
Representation, exclusive, 103–4
Reproductive hazards, 28–29, 33–39; exclusionary policies and, 20–21; identification with women, 19–20
Reproductive rights, 10–14, 39
Research: control and/or suppression of, 48–49; occupational health, 43–44
Richardson, Elliot, 85
Rights: categories of, 8–9, 124–31; central role of, 131–35; conflicting, 136–37, 140; development of, 126, 135–36; disputes over, 126–31; legal recognition of, 134–35; limitations of, 136–39; nature of, 125, 131; *See also* Strike rights; Union rights
Right-to-a-job, 57, 75–84; as property right, 76–84
Right-to-know, 39–55; arguments against, 49–53; components of, 39–48; informed consent and, 28, 33; issue behind, 53
Right-to-refuse, 57, 61–74; conditions necessary for, 66; employer response to, 61–72; legal status in U.S. of, 72–74; systematic response to, 71
"Right-to-work" laws, 90–91, 96, 98–99
Runaway shops: solutions to, 94–95; threat of, 76–81

Safety campaigns, corporate, 42–43
Safety hazards. *See* Occupational hazards
Sandel, Michael, 133–34, 138, 139
Saskatchewan, Canada, 63–64
Schwartz, Adina, 85
Scott, Rachel, 59, 65
Secondary boycotts, 97–98
Self-determination, 55–56, 70, 85–86, 127
Sex discrimination. *See* Exclusionary policies; Protective policies
Shue, Henry, 129–30
Shutdown, threat of, 76–81
Silica dust hazards, 59
Small Business Administration, 77
Social relations, 125, 131
Song of the Canary (film), 28
Sovereignty, doctrine of, 108–11
Spencer, Charles, 65
Spero, Sterling, 108–9
Sperry Rand Corporation, 77
Staub, Susan, 103, 104
Steel industry hazards, 58–61
Stellman, Jeanne, 19
Sterilization: abuse, 13–14; exclusionary policies and, 5–7; without informed consent, 34–38; workplace hazards and, 28–29, 33–39
Stewart, Potter, 73
Stress, heat, 60
Strike rights: defined, 71; essentiality of services and, 111–14; firefighters and police, 116–20; J. P. Stevens Co. and, 93–94; in public sector, 106–21; sympathy, 97–98
Substantive rights, 128–31
Supreme Court: interpretation of constitutional rights, 129; on right to refuse, 73; Wagner Act and, 93–95
Sweden: regulation of plant closings in, 78–79; right to refuse in, 64, 69
Sympathy strikes, 97–98

Taft-Hartley Act, 95–99; anti-communist measure in, 96–97
Textile industry: hazards of, 89–91; relocation of, 80
Textile Workers Union of America, 88
Title VII of the Civil Rights Act, 10, 27
Trade-secret argument, 50
Training in safety problems, 69
"Two Concepts of Liberty" (Berlin), 126

Unemployment, impact of, 83–84
Unfair labor practices: employer, 92–93; union, 97–99
Union(s): Communism and, 96–97; contracts, 65; cooperation between, 94; discriminatory membership policies, 104–6; medical record access of, 47–48; democratic participation in, 121–22; security, 98–105; unfair labor practices, 97–99
Union rights, 76, 87–122; history of development, 91–99; in public sector, 106–21; Wagner Act and, 92–95
Union shop, 96, 98–99, 105
United Farm Workers' Union, 31
United Kingdom, plant closings in, 78
United States Steel Corporation, 78
United Steelworkers of America, 78

Wage replacement, 82–85
Wagner Act, 71–72, 92–95
Weisenfeld, Allan, 120–21
West Germany, plant closings in, 78
Williams, Bernard, 128
Women's Work, Women's Health (Stellman), 19
Workers' compensation laws, 19
Workplace: control of, 53; research on, 43–44. *See also* Occupational hazards
Work stoppages, partial, 117